Mastering ChatGPT for Nonfiction Authors

Mastering ChatGPT for Nonfiction Authors

How to Use ChatGPT to Write a Book, Leveraging ChatGPT for Creating, Publishing & Selling Successful Non-Fiction Books

Mindscape Artwork Publishing
Mauricio Vasquez

Toronto, Canada

Authors: Mauricio Vasquez

First Printing: August 2024

ISBN-978-1-998402-68-7 (Paperback)
ISBN-978-1-998402-69-4 (Hardcover)
ISBN- 978-1-998402-70-0 (E-book)

Table of Contents

Chapter 1. Preface

In the ever-evolving world of digital publishing, the introduction of artificial intelligence, particularly ChatGPT, has transformed the way authors approach writing, research, and content creation. As an author, navigating this landscape requires not only creativity but also a strategic understanding of how to leverage these powerful tools effectively. This book is designed to guide you through the process of integrating ChatGPT into your writing workflow, providing you with a structured approach to unlock its full potential.

The structure of this book is meticulously crafted to ensure that you gain a comprehensive understanding of how to use ChatGPT effectively, regardless of your experience level. Each chapter is focused on a specific aspect of the writing and publishing process, breaking down the steps you need to follow to achieve optimal results. While some of these steps may appear in multiple chapters, this repetition is intentional. The consistent application of certain principles across different stages of your work is key to mastering ChatGPT's capabilities.

Each chapter in this book is organized into clear, actionable steps. You will begin by learning the foundational concepts necessary to interact with ChatGPT in a way that maximizes its utility. From there, you will progress through more specialized tasks, such as brainstorming ideas, conducting research, crafting compelling content, and engaging in effective book marketing. The structure of each chapter is designed to build upon the previous one, ensuring that you develop a solid, cohesive strategy for using ChatGPT in all facets of your work.

The reason for the overlap in steps between chapters is simple: the best results with ChatGPT come from providing it with relevant context, framed by a well-thought-out series of instructions. For instance, whether you are brainstorming ideas for your book, writing its content, or creating marketing materials, the steps you take to prepare your prompts—such as defining your goals, understanding your target audience, and organizing your thoughts—remain consistent. By reinforcing these steps across different applications, this book helps you internalize the process, making it second nature by the time you reach the final chapter.

This approach ensures that you not only understand how to use ChatGPT in isolated tasks but also appreciate how these tasks interconnect to form a holistic approach to writing and publishing. By following the structured steps outlined in each chapter, you will learn to create the right context for ChatGPT, allowing the AI to generate content that is not only relevant but also insightful, creative, and aligned with your goals.

In summary, this book is more than a guide—it is a roadmap to mastering ChatGPT in a way that enhances every aspect of your writing and publishing journey. By the end of this book, you will have developed a robust, repeatable process for using ChatGPT that can be applied to any writing project, ensuring that you achieve the best possible outcomes. I encourage you to engage with each chapter fully, understanding that the repetition of certain steps is designed to deepen your expertise and confidence in using this transformative tool.

As you move forward, remember that the key to success with ChatGPT lies in the details—providing clear, relevant context and following the structured steps will unlock the full potential of this AI, empowering you to take your writing to new heights.

Disclaimer: This book includes elements generated by the ChatGPT language model.

Chapter 2. Free Goodwill

Would you consider taking a minute to make a lasting impact on another writer's journey? Your experience and insights are invaluable.

Right now, there's an aspiring author, a content creator, or a professional looking to elevate their writing with AI. They're navigating the challenges of crafting engaging content, exploring new ideas, and perhaps even publishing their first book. Your review could be the guiding light they need.

Think of reviews as more than just feedback—they're endorsements, shared knowledge, and signals of trustworthiness. If this book has provided you with valuable insights or practical strategies, could you share your experience through a quick review? By doing so, you help to:

- Direct someone to tools and techniques that can enhance their writing with ChatGPT.
- Empower an individual to confidently navigate the world of AI-assisted authorship.
- Offer perspectives that others might not have considered, enriching their creative process.
- Spark transformation in another writer's approach, leading to success in their projects.

By reviewing this book, you contribute to expanding the possibilities of AI in writing for others. If you found value in these pages, please share it within your network. People often appreciate those who introduce them to valuable resources.

Enjoyed the book? Scan the QR code to quickly leave a review. Your feedback helps others on their writing journey!

Your support means a lot. Thank you for helping to shape the future of writing and creativity with AI.

We have something else for you!

In a world where AI is transforming every industry, harnessing the power of these tools is crucial to achieving success.

If you're ready to take your writing to the next level and make your first million with ChatGPT, this book is your roadmap.

Scan this QR code to access this book.

Chapter 3. Introduction

Welcome to "Mastering ChatGPT for Nonfiction Authors" a comprehensive guide that will introduce you to the transformative potential of ChatGPT. This powerful language model can revolutionize your writing process, whether you're a seasoned author or just starting out. This book aims to show you how to leverage ChatGPT to write better, faster, and more effectively.

Unveiling ChatGPT

First, let's demystify ChatGPT. The acronym "ChatGPT" stands for "Conversational Generative Pre-trained Transformer." Here's what that means:

- Chat: Highlights its capability to generate human-like text, making it suitable for conversational applications and book writing.

- GPT: Stands for "Generative Pre-trained Transformer," a machine learning model that excels in understanding and generating human language.

OpenAI, the pioneering company behind ChatGPT, is at the forefront of artificial intelligence research. Their mission is to ensure that AI benefits all of humanity. In addition to developing language models, OpenAI conducts research in various AI-related fields, including machine learning, robotics, and neuroscience.

How ChatGPT can transform your writing

ChatGPT operates as a sophisticated language model trained to predict the next word or phrase in a given context. This is achieved by feeding the model a vast dataset of human-generated text, enabling it to learn the intricacies of natural language. Once trained, ChatGPT can generate coherent, engaging text that is often indistinguishable from human writing.

One of ChatGPT's standout capabilities is its versatility. It can assist authors with brainstorming, idea generation, drafting, editing, and even proofreading by identifying errors and suggesting improvements. This makes ChatGPT an invaluable tool throughout the entire writing process.

Why embrace ChatGPT?

Here are some compelling reasons why authors should embrace ChatGPT:

1. Time-saving

One of the most significant advantages of using ChatGPT is the time it saves throughout the writing process. Here are a few ways it accomplishes this:

- Automated drafting: ChatGPT can quickly produce initial drafts based on your outlines or prompts, significantly reducing the time it takes to get your ideas down on paper.

- Efficient editing: The model can instantly identify and suggest corrections for grammatical errors, awkward phrasing, and structural issues, saving you hours of painstaking editing.

- Rapid research: ChatGPT can provide summaries and insights on a wide range of topics, helping you gather the information you need without spending countless hours on research.

2. Creativity boost

ChatGPT can serve as a powerful catalyst for creativity, helping you break through writer's block and infuse your work with fresh ideas:

- Idea generation: By providing prompts or asking for suggestions, you can receive a flood of creative ideas, whether you need a plot twist, a unique setting, or a compelling character backstory.

- Inspiration for style and tone: If you're struggling to find the right voice for your writing, ChatGPT can generate text in various styles and tones, offering you a template to build upon.

- Diverse perspectives: ChatGPT's ability to draw from a vast dataset of human-generated text means it can introduce new perspectives and unconventional ideas that you might not have considered.

3. Versatility

ChatGPT's versatility makes it an invaluable tool for every stage of the writing and publishing process:

- Content creation: Beyond drafting and brainstorming, ChatGPT can help you expand sections of your manuscript, add descriptive details, and ensure narrative coherence.

- Editing and proofreading: From simple grammatical corrections to more complex stylistic adjustments, ChatGPT can polish your text and make it more engaging and readable.

- Summarizing: If you need to condense large volumes of text, such as research articles or previous drafts, ChatGPT can generate concise summaries that capture the essential points.

- Marketing: ChatGPT can assist in crafting compelling marketing copy, social media posts, and book descriptions that resonate with your target audience. It can also generate ideas for blog posts, newsletters, and other promotional content.

4. Cost-effective solution

Hiring professional editors, proofreaders, and marketing experts can be expensive. ChatGPT provides a cost-effective alternative by offering many of these services through its AI capabilities. While it may not replace the nuanced touch of a human expert, it provides a high-quality and affordable supplement to your writing process.

5. Consistency and quality control

Maintaining a consistent voice and style throughout a lengthy manuscript can be challenging. ChatGPT helps by:

- Ensuring uniformity: It can help maintain a consistent tone and style across different sections of your book, which is particularly useful if you are writing over an extended period.

- Quality checks: Regularly running your text through ChatGPT for feedback and corrections ensures a high standard of quality and minimizes the risk of overlooked errors.

6. Accessibility and support

ChatGPT is accessible anytime and anywhere, providing you with constant support throughout your writing journey. Whether you're working late at night or need a quick answer during a weekend writing session, ChatGPT is always available to assist you.

- 24/7 Availability: Unlike human collaborators who may have limited availability, ChatGPT can provide immediate feedback and assistance whenever you need it.

- User-friendly: ChatGPT is designed to be intuitive and easy to use, making it accessible to authors of all technological proficiencies.

By embracing ChatGPT, authors can streamline their writing process, enhance their creativity, and improve the overall quality of their work. The combination of time-saving features, creative inspiration, and versatile capabilities makes ChatGPT an essential tool for modern writers looking to leverage technology to their advantage.

A journey through the capabilities of ChatGPT

Throughout this book, we will delve into the numerous capabilities of ChatGPT, exploring how it can be integrated into various stages of the writing process. We will cover:

- Brainstorming and idea generation: ChatGPT can help overcome writer's block by providing a wealth of ideas based on a simple prompt. Whether you need a plot twist, a character background, or a list of potential topics for a chapter, ChatGPT can generate diverse and innovative suggestions. This feature is particularly useful when you're at the initial stages of your project and need a creative boost to get started.

- Drafting and writing: Once you have a clear idea of what you want to write, ChatGPT can assist in drafting your content. By inputting your outline or key points, you can receive a well-structured and fluid narrative that maintains your voice and style. ChatGPT can help you expand on brief points, add descriptive details, and ensure that your writing flows naturally from one section to the next.

- Editing and proofreading: Editing is a critical part of the writing process, and ChatGPT excels in this area. It can review your text for grammatical errors, awkward phrasing, and inconsistencies. By suggesting improvements and corrections, ChatGPT helps refine your manuscript, making it more polished and professional. Additionally, it can rephrase sentences to enhance clarity and readability, ensuring that your message is conveyed effectively.

- Research assistance: If your writing requires factual accuracy or background information, ChatGPT can assist with research. By providing summaries of complex topics or suggesting reliable sources, ChatGPT can help you gather the necessary information to support your arguments and enrich your narrative. This feature saves you time and ensures that your content is well-informed and credible.

- Stylistic adjustments: Depending on your audience and purpose, you may need to adjust the tone and style of your writing. ChatGPT can adapt its output to match different styles, whether you need a formal academic tone, a conversational blog post, or a compelling marketing copy. This flexibility ensures that your writing resonates with your intended readers and meets the standards of your genre or field.

- Consistency and coherence: Maintaining consistency in tone, style, and content can be challenging, especially in long manuscripts. ChatGPT can help you keep track of character traits, plot points, and thematic elements, ensuring that your writing remains coherent throughout. It can also assist in aligning different sections of your book, making sure that transitions are smooth and logical.

- Multilingual capabilities: For authors working on multilingual projects or targeting a global audience, ChatGPT's ability to understand and generate text in multiple languages is invaluable. It can translate content, help you maintain linguistic accuracy, and adapt your writing to different cultural contexts, broadening your reach and appeal.

- Feedback and iteration: Finally, ChatGPT can serve as a valuable feedback tool. By reviewing your work and providing constructive criticism, it helps you identify areas for improvement. You can iterate on your drafts, refining and enhancing your content until it meets your standards of excellence. This iterative process ensures that your final manuscript is of the highest quality.

Overall, ChatGPT's versatility and advanced language capabilities make it an indispensable tool for authors. By integrating ChatGPT into your writing process, you can enhance your productivity, creativity, and precision, ultimately producing a more polished and compelling book.

Ethical considerations and best practices

While ChatGPT offers tremendous potential, it is essential to approach its use thoughtfully. This book will also address the ethical considerations and limitations of using AI in writing. We will provide guidelines to ensure that you use ChatGPT responsibly and effectively.

Your companion in the writing journey

By the end of this book, you will have a thorough understanding of how to harness the power of ChatGPT to enhance your writing process. Whether you are generating fresh ideas, crafting compelling narratives, or refining your manuscripts, ChatGPT will be your invaluable ally in your writing journey.

Get ready to embark on an exciting journey that will transform your approach to writing. Let's dive into the world of ChatGPT and discover how this cutting-edge technology can help you achieve your writing goals.

Chapter 4. Getting Started with ChatGPT

To begin using ChatGPT, follow these simple steps:

STEP 1: Sign up for an OpenAI account

Go to chat.openai.com and sign up for an OpenAI account. This will provide you with access to ChatGPT.

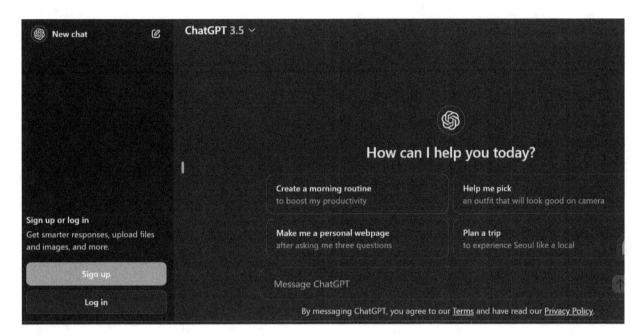

To get started with an account, just navigate to the OpenAI website and select the 'Sign Up' option. During the registration process, you'll be asked to enter basic details like your name and email address, or sign up with your Google, Microsoft or Apple account, and to accept the terms of service. After you've finished these steps, you'll have your new account ready, and you can log in to explore.

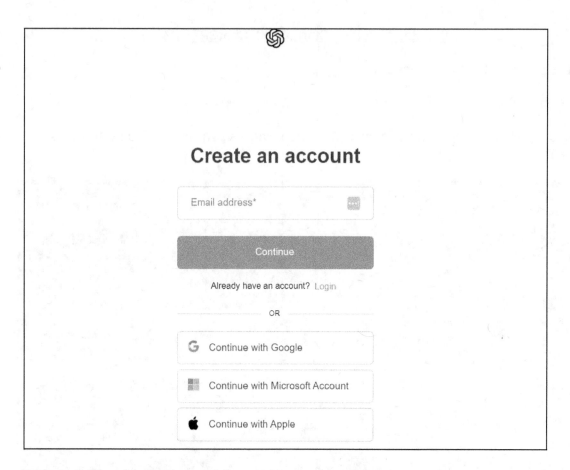

STEP 2: Select your GPT model (for paid accounts only)

Upon registering for ChatGPT, there's an option to upgrade to 'ChatGPT Plus' at $20 a month. A key advantage is uninterrupted access to ChatGPT, even when the free version reaches capacity limits.

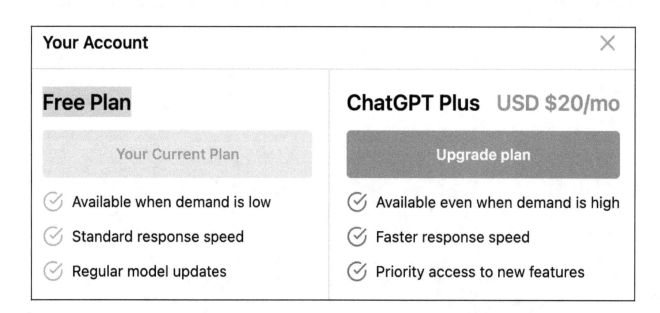

As a ChatGPT Plus user, especially with the introduction of the latest GPT model, you'll find an additional feature: a dropdown menu at the top of the interface, allowing you to select from different models. Opting for the latest GPT model is recommended for optimal results, though we note it comes normally with a limit of 25 messages every three hours. ChatGPT Plus subscription gives you access to GPTs. More on GPTs in a subsequent chapter.

STEP 3: Engage with the ChatGPT model

After logging in at chat.openai.com, you're ready to interact with the ChatGPT model. Just enter your query in the input field and hit the 'Send' button. ChatGPT will craft a response tailored to your prompt.

Try various prompts and adjust the settings to observe different responses from ChatGPT. You might, for instance, alter the length and tone to gauge their impact on the uniqueness and imaginative quality of the responses. Enter your prompts in the designated area marked "Message ChatGPT".

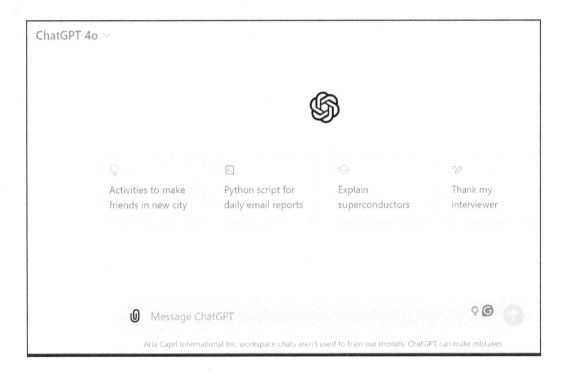

STEP 4: ChatGPT in real-time use

Below is an example of ChatGPT in use. You can see a prompt I entered: This is how the ChatGPT interface appears; I encourage you to explore it at chat.openai.com.

- Example Prompt: *"I recently purchased a book on how to use ChatGPT for writing nonfiction books. What recommendations do you have for getting the most out of it?"*

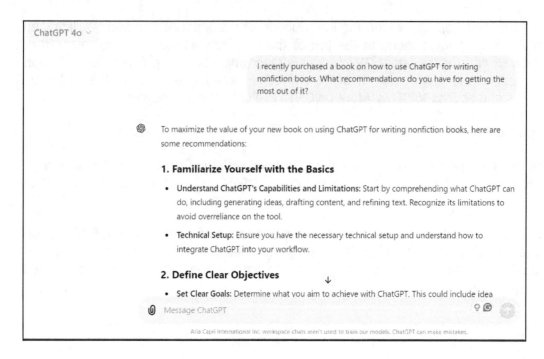

You can start with a basic prompt, probe it with questions, or challenge it with tasks like rewriting their output in a simpler language, translating, analyzing data, summarizing books, suggesting readings, and even brainstorming questions to ask ChatGPT itself.

For optimal utilization of this book, I suggest you employ the prompt that I previously showed and adapt it to your circumstances. This approach will ensure you derive maximum benefit from the contents of the book.

You can basically ask ChatGPT whatever you would like to know or learn. You literally have the entire world's knowledge at our fingertips.

Chapter 5. ChatGPT Prompts

Prompts are the key to unlocking the full potential of ChatGPT. They are suggestions, questions, or ideas that guide the chatbot's responses. For ChatGPT to provide helpful and accurate responses, it needs well-crafted prompts with background information and relevant data.

Becoming proficient at writing effective prompts takes time and experience, but by following some best practices, you can achieve success quickly:

1. Be precise in your instructions

Precision is crucial when crafting prompts, especially if you are using ChatGPT to assist with writing nonfiction books. Clear and concise instructions help ChatGPT understand your goals, tone, and scope.

Example:

- Example Prompt: *"Generate ideas for a nonfiction book."*

    - Outcome: ChatGPT might provide a broad range of book ideas that may not align with your specific interests or target audience.

- Precise Example Prompt: *"Generate nonfiction book ideas about self-care and wellness tailored for young adults."*

    - Outcome: ChatGPT will produce focused, relevant book ideas specifically aimed at self-care and wellness for young adults.

2. Integrate contextual information

Incorporating relevant context into your prompts enhances the accuracy of ChatGPT's responses. Providing background information about your book's theme, audience, or objectives can lead to more tailored and effective outputs.

Example:

- Basic Example Prompt: *"Suggest book titles."*

    - Outcome: ChatGPT may offer generic book titles.

- Contextual Example Prompt: *"Suggest book titles for a nonfiction book about self-care and wellness tailored for young adults."*

    - Outcome: ChatGPT will generate titles specifically suited to the topic of self-care and wellness.

3. Segment your interactions

For complex tasks, breaking them down into simpler prompts can make the process more manageable and efficient. Dividing the task into sections allows ChatGPT to focus on one part at a time, ensuring thorough and detailed responses.

Example:

- Complex Prompt: *"Write a chapter on using ChatGPT for research."*

  - Outcome: The response may lack depth or structure.

- Segmented Prompts:

  - *"Write an introduction for a chapter on using ChatGPT for research in nonfiction writing."*

  - *"Explain how ChatGPT can help identify reliable sources of information."*

  - *"Describe how to use ChatGPT to organize and synthesize research findings."*

  - *"Conclude the chapter with tips on verifying the accuracy of information obtained through ChatGPT."*

    - Outcome: Each section is crafted in detail, resulting in a comprehensive and well-structured chapter.

4. Continuous refinement

Use ChatGPT's initial outputs as a foundation, then refine and personalize them to align with your unique voice and objectives. This iterative process ensures the content remains relevant and specific to your needs.

Example:

- Initial Example Prompt: *"Draft an introduction to a book on using ChatGPT for writing nonfiction."*

  - Outcome: A general introductory passage.

- Refinement Example Prompt: *"Draft an introduction to a book on using ChatGPT for writing nonfiction highlighting the benefits of using ChatGPT for brainstorming, drafting, and editing in the nonfiction writing process."*

  - Outcome: A more polished and targeted introduction that highlights key benefits.

5. Employ follow-up prompts

To gain deeper insights and more detailed responses, use follow-up prompts based on ChatGPT's initial answers. This approach allows you to expand on specific points and enrich the content further.

Example:

- Initial Example Prompt: *"List the benefits of using ChatGPT for nonfiction authors."*

    - Outcome: A list of benefits.

- Follow-Up Example Prompt: *"Provide detailed explanations for each benefit, focusing on how ChatGPT can improve productivity, creativity, and accuracy for nonfiction authors."*

    - Outcome: In-depth explanations that enhance the initial list and provide greater value.

By applying these best practices, you can effectively harness the power of ChatGPT to produce high-quality, relevant content for your nonfiction writing projects. Precision, context, segmentation, refinement, and follow-up prompts are key strategies that will help you get the most out of this powerful tool.

As you continue to practice and refine your prompt-writing skills, you'll find that ChatGPT becomes an indispensable ally in your writing and self-publishing endeavors.

Important note for your reference:

The prompts in this book are straightforward and designed for efficient learning. They are basic and to the point, ensuring that you can grasp the concepts quickly. However, we highly recommend reviewing the 39 best practices for ChatGPT prompts included in Appendix 1. These best practices will equip you with the knowledge to craft more powerful prompts, crucial for advanced writing tasks and for getting the most out of ChatGPT in your book-writing journey.

Chapter 6. Prompt Frameworks

Harnessing the power of ChatGPT requires more than just random prompts; it demands strategic prompt engineering for optimal results. This chapter introduces a set of innovative frameworks that will enhance your interaction with ChatGPT, ensuring you craft each prompt to produce the most effective and customized responses.

Each framework is a toolset that instructs ChatGPT not only on what to answer but also on how to shape that answer to fit your unique requirements.

1. R-T-F (Role-Task-Format)

The R-T-F framework is a foundational structure that guides ChatGPT by defining a specific role, a task to be accomplished, and the preferred format for the response.

- Role: Act as a [specific professional or expert].

- Task: Create [a specific deliverable or outcome].

- Format: Show as [the desired format for the response].

Example:

If you're writing a nonfiction book and need an expert to help draft a chapter introduction:

- Example Prompt: *"Act as an experienced nonfiction author. Write an engaging introduction for a chapter on using AI tools like ChatGPT to enhance writing productivity for self-publishing authors. Format the introduction as a compelling narrative with key benefits highlighted in bullet points."*

    - Role: Act as an experienced nonfiction author.

    - Task: Write an engaging introduction for a chapter on using AI tools like ChatGPT to enhance writing productivity.

    - Format: Format the introduction as a compelling narrative with key benefits highlighted in bullet points.

2. T-A-G (Task-Action-Goal)

T-A-G sharpens the focus by defining a straightforward task, the action ChatGPT should take, and the overarching goal.

- Task: Determine what requires evaluation or creation.

- Action: State the action ChatGPT must undertake.

- Goal: Clarify the desired outcome or objective.

Example:

For an author looking to improve their book's structure:

- Example Prompt: *"Act as a professional book editor. Review the table of contents for my nonfiction book on using AI for writing and provide suggestions to enhance its logical flow and coherence."*
    - Task: Review the table of contents for a nonfiction book.
    - Action: Provide suggestions to enhance its logical flow and coherence.
    - Goal: Ensure the book's structure is logical and coherent.

3. B-A-B (Before-After-Bridge)

B-A-B navigates from the current challenge to the desired future state, outlining the steps to get there.

- Before: Explain the problem or current situation.
- After: State the desired outcome or future state.
- Bridge: Ask for the steps to connect 'Before' to 'After'.

Example:

For authors struggling with book marketing:

- Example Prompt: *"Act as a book marketing expert. Analyze the current limited reach of my self-published nonfiction book on AI writing tools (Before) and develop a comprehensive marketing plan to increase its visibility and sales (After). Outline the key strategies and steps to achieve this goal (Bridge)."*
    - Before: Analyze the current limited reach of my self-published nonfiction book.
    - After: Develop a comprehensive marketing plan to increase visibility and sales.
    - Bridge: Outline the key strategies and steps to achieve this goal.

4. C-A-R-E (Context-Action-Result-Example)

C-A-R-E incorporates comprehensive context to craft targeted actions and expected results, supported by examples.

- Context: Provide the background or setting for the task.
- Action: Describe the targeted action to be taken.
- Result: Clarify the anticipated outcome.
- Example: Give examples to illustrate the desired result.

Example:

For launching a new book:

- Example Prompt: *"Act as a book launch strategist. Develop a launch strategy for my nonfiction book on using ChatGPT for writing productivity. The strategy should aim to boost pre-orders and online engagement (Context). Create a detailed plan with actionable steps for social media campaigns, email marketing, and influencer partnerships (Action). The goal is to achieve high visibility and strong pre-order numbers (Result). Here is an example of a successful book launch: [Insert example of a successful book launch] (Example)."*

    - Context: Develop a launch strategy for a nonfiction book on using ChatGPT for writing productivity.

    - Action: Create a detailed plan with actionable steps for social media campaigns, email marketing, and influencer partnerships.

    - Result: Achieve high visibility and strong pre-order numbers.

    - Example: Insert example of a successful book launch.

5. R-I-S-E (Role-Input-Steps-Expectation)

R-I-S-E framework focuses on establishing a role for ChatGPT, detailing the input required, delineating the steps for the task, and setting clear expectations for the outcome.

- Role: Assign a specific role for ChatGPT to embody.

- Input: Detail the information or data that will inform ChatGPT's actions.

- Steps: Lay out the procedural steps ChatGPT should follow to accomplish the task.

- Expectation: Clearly articulate the results you expect from ChatGPT's efforts.

Example:

For crafting a book proposal:

- Example Prompt: *"Act as an experienced literary agent. Given the outline and key points of my nonfiction book on leveraging ChatGPT for writing (Input), create a step-by-step book proposal that includes a compelling summary, market analysis, and target audience description (Steps). The proposal should be designed to attract potential publishers and agents (Expectation)."*

    - Role: Act as an experienced literary agent.

    - Input: Given the outline and key points of my nonfiction book on leveraging ChatGPT for writing.

- ○ Steps: Create a step-by-step book proposal that includes a compelling summary, market analysis, and target audience description.

- ○ Expectation: Attract potential publishers and agents.

Best practices to work with prompt frameworks

When learning about and applying the ChatGPT prompt frameworks to craft effective prompts, consider the following:

1. Understand each framework thoroughly: Before applying a framework, ensure you have a deep understanding of its components and the purpose it serves. Each framework—be it R-T-F, T-A-G, B-A-B, C-A-R-E, or R-I-S-E—streamlines specific types of interactions with ChatGPT.

   Familiarize yourself with examples and experiment with each element to see how it affects the AI's response. Understanding the nuances will help you choose the right framework for your needs.

2. Start with clear and concise prompts: Simplicity is key when beginning to use these frameworks. Start with prompts that are direct and to the point. This will make it easier for you to evaluate the effectiveness of the framework and the AI's response.

   As you gain confidence, you can gradually introduce complexity by adding more context, nuances, or creative angles to your prompts. This iterative process of starting simple and slowly adding complexity helps in building a solid foundation for advanced prompt engineering.

3. Iterate and refine based on feedback: Use the responses you receive from ChatGPT as feedback to refine your prompts. If the output isn't what you expected, tweak your prompt by adjusting the role, task, action, or other components within the framework.

   This cycle of iteration and refinement is crucial—it not only improves the quality of your prompts over time, but also enhances your understanding of how ChatGPT interprets and responds to different instructions.

By including these considerations in your learning process, you will become more capable of effectively using the prompt frameworks. This will lead to more precise and useful interactions with ChatGPT, ultimately enhancing your productivity, creative output, and overall success in writing and self-publishing nonfiction books.

Chapter 7. Why Start Writing Now

Embarking on your book-writing journey early offers numerous personal and professional benefits. Here, we explore eight compelling reasons to begin writing books, highlighting the invaluable advantages this pursuit can bring to your life.

Embarking on your book-writing journey early offers numerous personal and professional benefits. Writing is not just about putting words on paper; it's about sharing your voice, experiences, and knowledge with the world. Every person has a unique perspective that can inspire, educate, and influence others. By starting to write now, you open the door to countless opportunities for growth, creativity, and impact.

Think about the stories that have shaped your life—the books that have offered solace during difficult times, sparked your imagination, or provided the knowledge to overcome challenges. Imagine being able to offer that same gift to others. The sooner you begin, the sooner you can start building a legacy that will resonate with readers for years to come.

1. Maximize your time

Time is our most precious resource. Starting to write books early allows you to accumulate experience, develop skills, and build an impressive body of work over time. The earlier you start, the more time you have to experiment with different styles, genres, and themes, ultimately honing your craft and finding your unique voice.

For instance, if you begin your writing journey at 30, by the age of 40, you could have a robust portfolio of works. This extensive collection not only showcases your growth as a writer but also makes it easier to attract publishers and build a dedicated readership. A decade of consistent writing can significantly enhance your credibility and visibility in the literary world.

2. Establish your personal brand

Writing early helps you establish a personal brand and carve out your place in the market, regardless of the field or topic you choose to write about. Early establishment of your brand allows you to become a recognizable figure, making it easier to connect with your target audience and build a loyal following.

Take J.K. Rowling, for example. Her success with the Harry Potter series not only made her a household name but also enabled her to expand into other creative ventures such as screenwriting and philanthropy. By starting early, you can similarly create a strong foundation for a multifaceted career.

3. Share knowledge and experience

Books provide a platform to share your knowledge and experiences with readers. Through your writing, you can become a mentor and guide, offering valuable insights that can help many in their personal and professional lives. Your words have the power to inspire and educate others, creating a ripple effect of positive change.

Dale Carnegie's "How to Win Friends and Influence People," published in 1936, is a prime example of this. The book has imparted timeless communication lessons to millions worldwide, proving that sharing your wisdom can have a lasting impact.

4. Generate a sustainable income

Writing books is an excellent way to generate a steady income. Great books can bring royalties, publishing deals, and related opportunities, contributing to long-term financial stability. As you build your portfolio and readership, the financial rewards can become increasingly significant, providing a reliable source of income.

Vietnamese author Nguyễn Nhật Ánh exemplifies this. He has built a stable income from writing books and other creative endeavors like screenplays and music. His success shows that with dedication and creativity, writing can be a lucrative career.

5. Expand your network

Writing and sharing your knowledge draws attention from peers, experts, and readers. This broadens your network, providing new collaboration opportunities and enhancing your career prospects. Engaging with a wide range of individuals can lead to fruitful partnerships and professional growth.

Tony Robbins, for instance, has connected with numerous successful entrepreneurs and industry leaders through his books. Hosting events that promote learning and networking, he has created a vast network that supports his various ventures.

6. Develop skills and persistence

Writing a book demands persistence and dedication. This process hones your writing, creative thinking, and resilience, significantly supporting your personal and professional growth. The challenges you face and overcome while writing can make you a more disciplined and determined individual.

Malcolm Gladwell refined his creative writing and analytical skills through his books, producing works that have garnered critical acclaim and wide readership. His journey illustrates how the discipline of writing can lead to exceptional personal and professional development.

7. Achieve pride and fulfillment

Completing a book and seeing it appreciated by readers brings immense pride and satisfaction. You contribute a part of yourself to the world, leaving a personal legacy. The joy of having your work acknowledged and valued is unparalleled, fostering a sense of accomplishment.

Nguyễn Phan Quế Mai, author of "The Mountains Sing," expressed her pride and joy in seeing her work loved and celebrated globally. Her experience highlights the profound fulfillment that comes from sharing your stories with the world.

8. Create a cultural legacy

Books add cultural value and become a legacy for future generations. Your works can educate, inspire, and leave a lasting impact on society. Writing allows you to contribute to the cultural and intellectual heritage of the world, influencing minds for years to come.

Nguyễn Nhật Ánh's literary creations, such as "Mắt biếc" and "Give Me a Ticket to Childhood," have become cultural treasures in Vietnam. These works educate and inspire generations, demonstrating the lasting legacy that books can create.

Starting your book-writing journey today allows you to explore these incredible benefits. Writing books not only enhances your personal and professional life but also leaves a lasting legacy for future generations. Embrace the opportunity, and you will surely not regret it.

Chapter 8. Crafting an Engaging Book

This chapter serves as an overarching guide that briefly introduces each step, emphasizing the integration of ChatGPT into the book creation process. More detailed discussions on specific topics are covered in other sections of the book. This approach helps provide a comprehensive overview while directing you to deeper insights elsewhere in the book.

Creating a high-quality and engaging book requires a strategic approach. Here are the essential steps, enriched with specific prompts you can use with ChatGPT to guide you through the process.

Step 1: Research and identify the right niche market and profitable topics for your book

The purpose of this step is to ensure that your book targets a specific audience with a keen interest in a topic, increasing the likelihood of reader engagement and sales.

To identify your interests, start by making a list of niche markets you're passionate about, such as health and beauty, travel, education, business, and marketing. Reflect on your expertise and interests to choose a niche that aligns with your knowledge and enthusiasm.

- Example Prompt: *"Act as a market researcher. Identify and list the top trending niche markets for nonfiction books in 2024, highlighting their growth potential and popularity."*

Using ChatGPT for research can help you analyze trends, competitiveness, and profitability of each niche. Ask for data on market size, growth potential, and existing competition.

- Example Prompt: *"Act as a market analyst. Provide a detailed analysis of current trends and profitable topics in the health and wellness niche for 2024, including data on market size and competition."*

Here are some example prompts to identify niche-related areas to explore deeply:

- *"Act as a market trend analyst. Identify which niche markets are experiencing the fastest growth in 2024 and explain why."*
- *"Act as a market strategist. Suggest profitable and engaging topics within the health niche that can attract readers and generate sales."*
- *"Act as a nonfiction book consultant. List five potential topics in the health niche that are engaging and profitable for nonfiction books."*

Step 2: Analyze customer profiles, content direction, and market research

The purpose of this step is to ensure that your book content is tailored to your target audience's needs, preferences, and expectations, which enhances reader satisfaction and engagement.

To understand your readers, create detailed customer profiles that include demographics, interests, lifestyle, needs, and expectations.

- Example Prompt: *"Act as a marketing expert. Create a detailed customer profile for a nonfiction book about self-care aimed at young adults, considering factors like gender, age, profession, income, interests, and lifestyle."*

Choosing a topic based on reader demographics and your interests helps ensure it meets your audience's needs.

- Example Prompt: *"Act as a content strategist. Suggest unique and engaging topics for a nonfiction book that would appeal to young adults interested in self-care."*

Conduct market research to ensure your topic is in demand and has potential by analyzing existing books, reader reviews, and market data.

- Example Prompt: *"Act as a market researcher. Conduct a detailed market analysis for a nonfiction book on effective time management skills and identify existing gaps and opportunities in the market."*

Step 3: Research and gather information

The purpose of this step is to build the foundation of your book with accurate and relevant information, ensuring the content is credible, informative, and valuable to readers.

To seek accurate, reliable sources, use books, magazines, articles, research reports, and credible online sources. Ensure your sources are up-to-date and reputable.

- Example Prompt: *"Act as a research assistant. Compile a list of credible sources and recent studies on effective time management techniques."*

Organize your research by noting and compiling important information, categorizing it according to different parts of the book. Use tools like spreadsheets or digital note-taking apps.

- Example Prompt: *"Act as an information organizer. Help me categorize information on time management into sections such as theory, techniques, and practical applications."*

Step 4: Plan and structure your book

The purpose of this step is to provide a clear and logical flow of information, making it easier for readers to follow and understand the content.

Outline the structure by determining the main parts of the book, such as the introduction, main content (divided into chapters), conclusion, and appendices. Create a detailed outline to guide your writing process.

- Example Prompt: *"Act as a book editor. Create a comprehensive outline for a nonfiction book on time management, including an introduction, main chapters, and a conclusion."*

Create an engaging introduction that introduces issues, questions, or unique perspectives to spark readers' curiosity and set the tone for the book.

- Example Prompt: *"Act as a writer. Draft an engaging introduction for a chapter on time management that highlights its importance and sets the stage for the rest of the book."*

Step 5: Draft the content

The purpose of this step is to create the main body of your book, ensuring the content is clear, informative, and engaging for readers.

Follow the structure by writing content according to the outlined structure using clear, understandable language, and avoiding overuse of jargon. Focus on making your writing accessible and engaging.

- Example Prompt: *"Act as a nonfiction author. Write the content for Chapter 2: Time Management Techniques using clear and accessible language."*

Incorporate examples and illustrations by using real-life examples, case studies, and illustrations to make it easier for readers to visualize and grasp the content.

- Example Prompt: *"Act as a case study writer. Provide real-life examples and case studies of effective time management in the workplace."*

Diversify content by combining text, images, graphs, and charts to engage readers and provide multiple ways to understand the information.

- Example Prompt: *"Act as a visual content creator. Suggest ways to visually represent time management techniques using graphs and charts."*

Step 6: Translate and edit

The purpose of this step is to polish and professionalize your book, improving readability, accuracy, and overall quality.

Edit for accuracy and flow by ensuring linguistic accuracy, and checking for spelling, grammar, and logical flow. Revise your draft to improve clarity and coherence.

- Example Prompt: *"Act as a copy editor. Review this chapter on time management for grammar and clarity, and suggest improvements for better flow. Here is the chapter: [Insert chapter's content]"*

Format and present your book by choosing appropriate fonts, colors, and font sizes, ensuring consistency throughout. Ensure all images and graphs are clear and appropriately placed.

- Example Prompt: *"Act as a book designer. Suggest a professional and reader-friendly format for an eBook on time management."*

Step 7: Design your book cover

The purpose of this step is to attract potential readers with a captivating cover that conveys the essence of your book, playing a crucial role in marketing and sales.

Choose relevant visuals by selecting appropriate images, colors, and fonts that are relevant to the topic and make a strong impression. The cover should be eye-catching and convey the essence of the book.

Here are a couple example prompts:

- *"Act as a graphic designer. Design a compelling book cover for an eBook on time management, including suggestions for color schemes and font styles."*
- *"Act as a professional graphic designer. Design a captivating book cover for a new book titled 'Mastering Time: Your Guide to Efficient Time Management.' The design should follow a blue color scheme and incorporate elements that evoke productivity, organization, and efficiency. Ensure the cover is visually appealing, professional, and suitable for both digital and print formats."* (Note that ChatGPT may have difficulty incorporating precise text into images. It is advisable to avoid providing the title to ChatGPT and instead, add it later using a design software tool.)

Step 8: Convert book format

The purpose of this step is to ensure your book is compatible with various e-readers and platforms, enhancing accessibility for readers.

Select a suitable format by choosing from common formats for books such as WORD, EPUB, MOBI, and PDF. Choose the format that best suits your distribution platform and audience.

- Example Prompt: *"Act as a digital publishing expert. Explain the advantages and disadvantages of different eBook formats like EPUB, MOBI, and PDF, and recommend the best format for a nonfiction book on time management."*

Use specialized software such as Calibre, Kindle Create, and Adobe InDesign to assist with eBook format conversion. Follow tutorials or seek professional help if needed.

- Example Prompt: *"Act as a tech support specialist. Guide me through converting a WORD document into an EPUB file using Calibre."*

Step 9: Promote and market your book

The purpose of this step is to reach your target audience, generate interest, and boost sales through effective promotion and marketing strategies.

Build a landing page by creating a dedicated page for your book that summarizes the content, showcases the cover, and includes author information. Make it easy for readers to purchase or download the book.

- Example Prompt: *"Act as a digital marketer. Create a landing page outline for promoting an book on time management, including key sections and elements to attract readers."*

Utilize social media by sharing information and purchase links on platforms like Facebook, Instagram, Twitter, and LinkedIn to attract readers. Use engaging posts, stories, and ads to promote your book.

- Example Prompt: *"Act as a social media manager. Draft a series of social media posts to promote a nonfiction eBook on time management, including sample text and images."*

Use email marketing by sending promotional emails about the book to your subscriber list, highlighting the benefits and features of the book. Personalize the emails to engage your audience.

- Example Prompt: *"Act as an email marketer. Write a promotional email for an eBook on time management to be sent to my subscriber list, emphasizing the book's value and unique insights."*

Step 10: Publish and sell your book

The purpose of this step is to choose the right publishing platform to reach your audience effectively and maximize sales.

Choose a publishing platform by researching and selecting from options such as Amazon Kindle Direct Publishing, Apple Books, Google Play Books, and Kobo Writing Life. Each platform has its own advantages and requirements.

- Example Prompt: *"Act as a publishing consultant. Compare the features and benefits of different book publishing platforms like Amazon KDP, Apple Books, and Google Play Books, and recommend the best option for a nonfiction book on time management."*

Chapter 9. Brainstorming with ChatGPT

Embarking on your book-writing journey can sometimes feel overwhelming, especially when it comes to brainstorming and generating fresh ideas. This chapter introduces how ChatGPT can be an invaluable ally in this process, providing diverse perspectives and stimulating creativity to enrich your nonfiction writing.

Enhancing the brainstorming process with ChatGPT

Brainstorming and idea generation are crucial steps in the writing process, particularly for nonfiction authors who need to present information clearly and logically. ChatGPT can significantly enhance this process by offering new angles and a plethora of ideas, ensuring your writing is both comprehensive and engaging.

By inputting a topic or theme into ChatGPT, you can receive a wealth of suggestions that explore multiple facets of your subject. This capability is especially beneficial for nonfiction writers who must cover their topics thoroughly while keeping their readers engaged.

For instance, if you are writing a nonfiction book about the history of the internet, you could ask ChatGPT to generate ideas for chapters or sections. ChatGPT might propose topics such as the early development of the internet, its societal impacts, or its role in the global economy.

Practical applications of ChatGPT in brainstorming

1. Generating chapter ideas

This step is essential because a well-structured book with clearly defined chapters helps in maintaining a logical flow and keeps the reader engaged from start to finish. By generating chapter ideas early in the process, you can create a detailed roadmap that guides your writing, making the entire process more manageable and focused.

- Example Prompt: *"Act as a historian and generate chapter ideas for a nonfiction book about the history of the internet."*

2. Creating writing prompts

Writing prompts serve as a catalyst for creativity, helping you to explore different aspects of your subject matter. They can prevent writer's block and ensure that your writing remains dynamic and interesting. By using writing prompts, you can delve deeper into topics, uncover new angles, and maintain a steady flow of ideas.

- Example Prompt: *"Act as a career coach and generate a list of 10 writing ideas about the topic of professional development suitable for a nonfiction book or article."*

3. Exploring alternative angles

Exploring alternative angles allows you to present your subject matter in a multifaceted way, appealing to a broader audience. This approach can reveal previously overlooked aspects of a topic, making your book more comprehensive and engaging. By considering different viewpoints, you can enrich your narrative and provide a well-rounded discussion of the subject.

- Example Prompt: *"Act as a nutritionist and generate a list of overlook topics related to nutrition and healthy eating for working mothers."*

Examples of effective Use of ChatGPT for brainstorming and idea generation

Example 1: Generating ideas for a book

This step is vital for aligning your book's content with the interests and needs of your target readers. A well-chosen title and theme can attract your intended audience, set clear expectations, and increase the book's marketability. By focusing on the right topics, you can ensure that your book addresses relevant issues and resonates with readers.

- Example Prompt: "Act as a financial advisor and generate ideas for a nonfiction book about personal finance for early-career employees."

Example 2: Generating ideas for a research article

This step is crucial for academic writing as it helps you to pinpoint significant issues worth investigating. By generating focused research prompts, you can develop articles that contribute to the academic community, fill knowledge gaps, and advance your field of study.

- Example Prompt: *"Act as a child psychologist and generate a list of 5 writing prompts related to the topic of parenting suitable for a research article in an academic journal."*

By leveraging ChatGPT for brainstorming and idea generation, you can overcome creative blocks and generate a wealth of ideas to enhance your nonfiction writing. Whether you need to develop chapter outlines, create engaging prompts, or explore new angles on a topic, ChatGPT can provide valuable assistance. Embrace this tool to streamline your brainstorming process, ensuring your nonfiction book is rich with insights and captivating content.

Chapter 10. Writing Trends & Styles

This chapter delves into the transformative power of ChatGPT, guiding you through the essential steps to leverage current book writing trends, styles, and methods. By integrating detailed prompts and best practices, you'll discover how to elevate your writing process, ensuring your nonfiction book resonates with readers and aligns with market demands.

Creating a high-quality and engaging book requires a strategic approach. Here are the essential steps you can use with ChatGPT to guide you through the process.

Step 1: Research and analyze current trends

Understanding current trends allows you to align your book with reader interests and market demands. By researching and analyzing these trends, you can identify popular genres, themes, and topics that are gaining traction. This insight helps you tailor your content to meet reader expectations, increasing the likelihood of your book's success.

- Example Prompt: *"Act as a literary market analyst. What are the current best-selling book trends for 2024?"*

Step 2: Explore writing styles and methods

Exploring different writing styles and methods enriches your storytelling toolkit. This variety allows you to experiment with new ways of presenting information, keeping your content fresh and engaging for readers. Understanding these styles helps you choose the most effective method to convey your message, making your writing more compelling.

- Example Prompt: *"Act as a writing coach. Describe some unique writing styles and methods for nonfiction books."*

Step 3: Generate ideas for your book

Generating ideas is the foundation of any writing project. Using ChatGPT to brainstorm ensures that you come up with innovative, relevant, and marketable ideas. This step helps you align your book's concept with current trends, ensuring it appeals to your target audience and stands out in a crowded market.

- Example Prompt: *"Act as a creative writing assistant. Based on current trends, generate ideas for a new nonfiction book on the topic of e-commerce."*

Step 4: Plan your book writing

A well-thought-out plan is crucial for the successful completion of your book. By outlining chapters, developing characters, and setting a timeline, you maintain focus and organization. This structured approach allows you to manage your time effectively, meet deadlines, and maintain consistency throughout your writing process.

- Example Prompt: *"Act as an experienced writing coach. Create a detailed guide on how to develop a well-thought-out plan for writing a book about the entertainment industry. This guide should cover the importance of outlining chapters, developing characters, and setting a timeline. Provide practical tips and examples to illustrate each point."*

Step 5: Drafting and editing

Drafting and editing are iterative processes that refine your ideas and improve your manuscript. Using ChatGPT for initial drafts and subsequent edits ensures clarity, coherence, and engagement. This step helps you enhance your writing quality, making your book more professional and polished.

- Example Prompt: *"Act as an editor. Help me edit and improve this paragraph using the chosen style and method. Here is the paragraph: [Insert paragraph]"*

Step 6: Reviews and feedback

Feedback is essential for identifying areas of improvement and ensuring your book meets high standards. ChatGPT can provide objective critiques, highlighting strengths and weaknesses. This feedback helps you refine your manuscript, making it more engaging and polished before final publication.

- Example Prompt: *"Act as a literary critic. Evaluate my book and give suggestions for improvement. Here is my book: [Insert the book's content]".*

Step 7: Preparing for publication

Preparing for publication involves finalizing the manuscript, finding a publisher, and planning a marketing strategy. ChatGPT can guide you through these steps, providing advice on submission processes, document preparation, and promotional tactics. This comprehensive preparation ensures your book is market-ready and positioned for success.

- Example Prompt: *"Act as a publishing consultant. Guide me through the steps to publish this book."*

Illustrative Example:

Here's an example of how you can use ChatGPT at each step:

1. Research and Analyze Current Trends

   ○ Example Prompt: *"Act as a market researcher. What are the emerging trends in the self-help book market for 2024?"*

2. Explore Writing Styles and Methods

   ○ Example Prompt: *"Act as a literary historian. Describe some unique writing styles and methods used in memoirs."*

3. Generate Ideas for Your Book

- Example Prompt: *"Act as an environmental scientist. Generate ideas for a nonfiction book about climate change solutions."*

4. Plan Your Book Writing

    - Example Prompt: *"Act as a strategic planner for authors. Help me outline a book on effective leadership in remote work environments."*

5. Drafting and Editing

    - Example Prompt: *"Act as a technical editor. Help me edit and improve this section on renewable energy technologies. Here is the section: [Insert the section]"*

6. Reviews and Feedback

    - Example Prompt: *"Act as a book critic. Review my draft chapter on the history of jazz music and suggest improvements."*

7. Preparing for Publication

    - *Example Prompt: "Act as a self-publishing consultant. Guide me through the steps to self-publish my book on digital marketing strategies."*

By following these outlined steps and applying the examples of ChatGPT prompts, you will easily utilize ChatGPT to support your book writing process, from exploring trends and styles to finalizing and publishing your work. This strategic approach ensures that your book is not only well-written but also aligns with current market trends and appeals to your target audience.

Chapter 11. Niche Research with ChatGPT

Embarking on the journey to become a bestselling author requires strategic planning, especially in discovering and identifying profitable niche markets and topics for your book. With the help of ChatGPT, you can streamline your research process, enhance content quality, and significantly boost your chances of success.

This chapter outlines essential steps, enriched with practical examples and prompts to help you leverage ChatGPT effectively.

Step 1: Define the niche market

This step helps you focus on specific areas with high demand and low competition, increasing the chances of your book's success. By understanding niche markets, you can tailor your content to meet the needs of a specific audience, making your book more appealing and marketable.

Begin by listing niche markets that interest you, such as health and beauty, travel, education, business, and marketing. Utilize ChatGPT to research and analyze trends, competition, and profitability within each niche.

- Example Prompt: *"Act as a market analyst. Identify the top three trending nonfiction niches for books in 2024."*

This helps you identify which niches have high demand and potential profitability.

Step 2: Formulate guiding questions

Developing specific questions helps to narrow down your research and gather targeted information that is crucial for making informed decisions about your niche and topics. Well-crafted questions direct ChatGPT to provide relevant and actionable insights, ensuring that your research is thorough and effective. This step also helps in uncovering new perspectives and opportunities within your chosen niche.

Identify prompts related to the niche market and topics you need to investigate. Clear and specific questions will provide more useful and targeted information.

- Example Prompts:
  - *"What are the most profitable topics within the personal development niche?"*
  - *"What are the key challenges faced by digital entrepreneurs?"*
  - *"What are the emerging trends in eco-friendly living?"*
  - *"Act as a trend researcher. What are the most profitable topics within the personal development niche, and what trends are emerging in eco-friendly living?"*

Step 3: Utilize ChatGPT for information gathering

Using ChatGPT to gather information saves time and provides a comprehensive view of current trends and data, enabling you to base your decisions on solid research. This ensures that the information you gather is up-to-date and relevant, which is crucial for staying competitive in the fast-paced book market. Additionally, leveraging ChatGPT's vast knowledge base helps you uncover insights that might not be readily available through traditional research methods.

Utilize the questions identified in Step 2 to ask ChatGPT for relevant information, data, and trends. Verify that the information collected is reliable and current.

- *Example Prompt: "Act as a market researcher. Provide recent trends and data on mental health topics within the personal development niche."*

This provides a foundation of current trends and profitable topics within your chosen niche.

Step 4: Analyze and evaluate the data

Analyzing and evaluating the gathered data helps you understand the potential of each niche and make an informed decision about the direction of your book. This step involves assessing the viability and sustainability of each niche based on factors such as market size, growth potential, and competition. By thoroughly evaluating the data, you can identify the most promising topics and ensure that your book addresses current demands and gaps in the market.

Collect, analyze, and assess the data from ChatGPT. Determine the characteristics, trends, and potential of each niche market and topic to make an appropriate selection.

- Example Prompt: *"Act as a data analyst. Summarize the key characteristics and trends of the most promising topics within the digital entrepreneurship niche."*

Use this summary to decide which topics are most promising for your eBook.

Step 5: Identify your target audience

Knowing your target audience is crucial for tailoring your content to their preferences and needs, ensuring higher engagement and satisfaction. This step involves creating detailed customer profiles to understand the demographics, interests, and behaviors of your potential readers. By identifying your target audience, you can craft content that resonates with them, leading to better reader retention and increased sales.

Using your analysis, identify the target audience for your book. This will help shape the content and writing style, ensuring it resonates with your readers.

- Example Prompt: *"Act as a marketing expert. Identify the target audience for a book on sustainable living practices."*

This helps you tailor your content to meet the needs and preferences of your target audience.

Step 6: Create content for the book

Creating compelling content involves brainstorming, drafting, and editing, all of which can be significantly enhanced using ChatGPT. This step ensures that your content is well-organized, engaging, and informative. By leveraging ChatGPT's capabilities, you can generate a wealth of ideas, refine your writing, and maintain a consistent tone and style throughout your book. This process also helps in addressing any potential gaps in your content, ensuring a comprehensive and valuable final product.

Utilize ChatGPT for brainstorming, drafting, and editing your book's content. Feel free to ask questions and engage in discussions with ChatGPT to achieve the best results.

- Example Prompt: *"Act as a creative writer. Help me brainstorm chapter ideas for an book on digital marketing strategies for small businesses."*

This provides a structured framework for your book.

Step 7: Optimize content and marketing

Optimizing content ensures it is engaging and valuable, while strategic marketing efforts help reach a wider audience and increase sales. This step involves refining your writing to enhance readability and coherence, as well as developing a comprehensive marketing strategy to promote your book. By optimizing both content and marketing, you can maximize the impact of your book and attract a loyal readership.

Use ChatGPT to refine your book's content, ensuring it is clear, engaging, and valuable to readers. Additionally, leverage ChatGPT's capabilities to plan effective marketing and promotional strategies.

- Example Prompt: *"Act as a marketing strategist. Suggest strategies to market a book on financial literacy for young adults."*

This ensures your book reaches a wider audience and attracts potential buyers.

Step 8: Review and adjust

Continuously reviewing and adjusting your book based on feedback ensures it remains relevant and meets readers' expectations. This step involves gathering feedback from various sources, analyzing it to identify common suggestions, and making necessary improvements to enhance the quality and appeal of your book. By regularly updating your content, you can maintain reader interest and ensure long-term success.

After completing and marketing your eBook, consistently monitor feedback from readers and the market. Use this feedback to make necessary adjustments and improvements.

- Example Prompt: *"Act as a feedback analyst. How can I gather and use feedback to improve my eBook on sustainable living practices?"*

Illustrative Examples

Example 1: Niche market "Holistic Health and Wellness"

Steps 1-3: Define the niche market, pose guiding questions, and seek information.

- *Example Prompt: "Act as a health and wellness expert. What are the current trends in holistic health, and what topics are most popular among readers?"*

Steps 4-5: Analyze, evaluate data, and identify the target audience.

- *Example Prompt: "Act as a market researcher. Summarize the target audience for a book on holistic health and wellness."*

Example 2: Niche market "Digital Marketing for Nonprofits"

Steps 1-3: Define the niche market, pose guiding questions, and seek information.

- *Example Prompt: "Act as a digital marketing consultant. What are the effective digital marketing strategies for nonprofits, and which topics are in high demand?"*

Steps 4-5: Analyze, evaluate data, and identify the target audience.

- *Example Prompt: "Act as a market analyst. Who is the target audience for a book on digital marketing for nonprofits?"*

Example 3: Niche market "Sustainable Fashion"

Steps 1-3: Define the niche market, pose guiding questions, and seek information.

- *Example Prompt: "Act as a fashion industry analyst. What are the latest trends in sustainable fashion, and what topics resonate most with consumers?"*

Steps 4-5: Analyze, evaluate data, and identify the target audience.

- *Example Prompt: "Act as a target market researcher. Identify the target audience for a book on sustainable fashion."*

Example 4: Niche market "Mindful Parenting"

Steps 1-3: Define the niche market, pose guiding questions, and seek information.

- Example Prompt: *"Act as a child psychologist. What are the benefits of mindful parenting, and what are the popular topics within this niche?"*

Steps 4-5: Analyze, evaluate data, and identify the target audience.

- Example Prompt: *"Act as a market analyst. Who is the target audience for an eBook on mindful parenting?"*

By following these outlined steps and applying the examples of ChatGPT prompts, you can effectively use ChatGPT to support your book writing process, from exploring trends and styles to finalizing and publishing your work. This strategic approach ensures that your book is not only well-written but also aligns with current market trends and appeals to your target audience.

Chapter 12. In-Depth Book Research

Writing a best-selling book can be a daunting task for any author. Fortunately, technological advancements have made researching and gathering information significantly easier. ChatGPT is a powerful tool that allows you to quickly and efficiently collect and synthesize information from a variety of sources.

Here are some secrets to effectively using ChatGPT for the research and information-gathering process of your eBook.

Step 1: Define the goal of your book

Clearly defining the goal and topic of your book helps ChatGPT focus on gathering relevant information and resources. A well-defined goal ensures that the information collected is pertinent and valuable for your writing. This clarity allows ChatGPT to streamline the search process, avoiding irrelevant data and honing in on what truly matters for your book. It sets the foundation for a focused, cohesive, and comprehensive book.

For example, if you are writing a book on stress reduction, clearly state your topic and use related keywords in your questions to narrow down ChatGPT's search scope.

- Example Prompt: *"Act as a research assistant. Search for books and articles on stress reduction techniques and mental health enhancement."*

Step 2: Use Accurate keywords for search

Using the correct keywords ensures that your search is accurate, yielding precise, actionable, and useful information relevant to your book's topic. Accurate keywords enhance the efficiency of the research process by filtering out unrelated information and zeroing in on high-quality, relevant data. This precision is crucial for building a strong, credible, and authoritative book.

For example, if you are looking for information on stress reduction, use related keywords like "meditation, yoga, relaxation, herbs, diet, exercise."

- Example Prompt: *"Act as an information specialist. Search for articles and resources on meditation techniques for stress reduction and mental health enhancement."*

Step 3: Utilize credible sources

Ensuring that the information gathered comes from credible sources guarantees the reliability and accuracy of your book's content. Using a variety of sources also enriches your book, providing multiple perspectives and a well-rounded view of the topic. Credibility is key to establishing trust with your readers and enhancing the overall quality of your work.

Use credible sources like reputable health organization websites, science websites, and expert experience-sharing databases.

- Example Prompt: *"Act as a content curator. Search for articles and resources from credible websites like WHO, Harvard Health Blog, and Psychology Today on the impact of yoga on mental health."*

Step 4: Intelligently use ChatGPT's search results

Synthesizing and organizing the information collected from ChatGPT helps in writing your book clearly and logically, making it easier for readers to understand the topic. Effective organization transforms raw data into a structured narrative, ensuring that your book is not only informative but also engaging and coherent. This step is crucial for maintaining reader interest and delivering a high-quality reading experience.

For example, arrange information on meditation techniques for stress reduction in increasing order of difficulty or divide them into smaller sections for easier reader access.

- Example Prompt: *"Act as an organizer. Summarize the benefits of yoga for mental health and stress reduction and group them as per their benefit type"*.

Best practices for using ChatGPT in research

- Verify Information: While ChatGPT is trained on a large dataset of human-generated text, it is crucial to verify the accuracy of the information it provides by cross-referencing with other sources.
- Refine Prompts: Be specific and clear in your prompts to get the most relevant and useful responses from ChatGPT.
- Iterate and Refine: Use ChatGPT iteratively, refining your questions and prompts to delve deeper into the subject matter and gather comprehensive information.

Illustrative Examples

Example 1: Researching "Weight Loss Through Plant-Based Diets"

Step 1-2: Define the niche and formulate guiding questions

- Example Prompt: *"Act as a dietitian. What are the most popular and effective plant-based diets currently?"*

Step 3: Utilize ChatGPT for information gathering

- Example Prompt: *"What are the benefits of losing weight through a plant-based diet?"*

Step 4: Analyze and evaluate data

- Example Prompt: *"Act as a market researcher. Summarize the target audience for an eBook on weight loss through plant-based diets."*

Example 2: Exploring "Learning English through Spatial Memory Techniques"

Step 1-2: Define the niche and formulate guiding questions

- Example Prompt: *"Act as an education expert. What are the current effective and unique methods for learning English?"*

Step 3: Utilize ChatGPT for information gathering

- Example Prompt: *"What are the benefits of using spatial memory techniques in learning English?"*

Step 4: Analyze and evaluate data

- Example Prompt: *"Act as a target market analyst. Identify the target audience for a book on learning English through spatial memory techniques."*

Writing the perfect book requires thorough research and the gathering of accurate and complete information. ChatGPT is a useful tool that saves time and effort in this process. By defining your book's goal, using accurate keywords, utilizing credible sources, and intelligently synthesizing search results, you can effectively use ChatGPT to research and gather information for your book.

Chapter 13. Customer Profiling & Market Research

In the current digital age, leveraging technology for customer profiling and market research is crucial for authors aspiring to write best-selling nonfiction books. ChatGPT offers a valuable tool to create accurate, up-to-date, and reliable customer profiles while conducting comprehensive market research.

Master the following steps to maximize the potential of ChatGPT in developing a deep understanding of your audience and the market landscape.

Step 1: Define your target audience

Understanding who your readers are is fundamental to creating content that appeals to them. By defining your target audience, you ensure your book is tailored to meet their interests and needs. This foundational step allows you to make informed decisions throughout the writing and marketing process, ensuring relevance and engagement.

- Example Prompt: *"Act as a market researcher. Define the target audience for a nonfiction book on sustainable living practices."*

This prompt helps you gather demographic and psychographic information about your potential readers.

Step 2: Use detailed demographics

Gathering detailed demographic information allows you to understand the age, gender, income, education, and other attributes of your audience. This helps in crafting content that resonates with them. Detailed demographics enable you to pinpoint exactly who will benefit from your book, allowing for targeted marketing strategies and personalized content creation.

- Example Prompt: *"Act as a demographic analyst. Provide detailed demographic information for readers of self-help books focused on career development."*

This response provides a clear picture of your audience's demographic profile.

Step 3: Analyze psychographic data

Psychographic data, including interests, values, attitudes, and lifestyles, provides deeper insights into your audience's motivations and behaviors. Understanding these elements helps you connect with your readers on a more personal level, creating content that speaks to their core values and aspirations.

- Example Prompt: *"Act as a psychographic analyst. Describe the psychographic profile of readers interested in mindfulness and meditation."*

This prompt helps you understand the inner motivations and preferences of your target audience.

Step 4: Identify pain points and needs

Knowing your audience's pain points and needs helps you address their challenges directly in your book, making it more relevant and valuable. Identifying and addressing these issues ensures that your book provides practical solutions, thereby increasing reader satisfaction and engagement.

- Example Prompt: *"Act as a consumer behavior analyst. Identify the main pain points and needs of individuals looking for financial independence."*

This insight allows you to tailor your content to solve specific problems your readers face.

Step 5: Determine content preferences

Understanding what type of content your audience prefers ensures that your book's style, format, and tone match their expectations. Catering to these preferences increases the likelihood of your book being well-received and widely recommended.

- Example Prompt: *"Act as a content strategist. What type of content do readers of personal finance books prefer?"*

This helps you align your book's format and style with your readers' preferences.

Step 6: Conduct comprehensive market research

Conducting thorough market research helps you understand the competitive landscape, identify gaps in the market, and spot emerging trends. This knowledge enables you to position your book strategically, offering unique insights that differentiate it from existing works.

- Example Prompt: *"Act as a market analyst. Provide an overview of the current market trends for nonfiction books on digital detox and identify potential gaps in the market."*

This step helps you position your book effectively within the market.

Step 7: Segment your audience

Segmenting your audience allows you to address specific sub-groups within your larger audience, making your book more personalized and impactful. Understanding these segments helps in creating targeted marketing campaigns and tailored content that speaks directly to the unique needs of each group.

- Example Prompt: *"Act as a market segment analyst. Segment the audience for a self-help book on achieving work-life balance."*

This helps you create targeted content for different segments of your audience.

Step 8: Create detailed customer personas

Customer personas are fictional characters that represent your ideal readers. They help you visualize and understand your audience better. Detailed personas guide your writing and marketing efforts, ensuring that all content is tailored to the specific characteristics and preferences of your target readers.

- Example Prompt: *"Act as a persona developer. Create detailed customer personas for a nonfiction book on leadership skills."*

This provides a clear, humanized picture of your ideal readers.

Step 9: Tailor your marketing strategy

Developing a marketing strategy based on your customer profiles ensures that your promotional efforts are effective and reach the right audience. A well-crafted strategy increases your book's visibility and appeal, leading to higher sales and engagement.

- Example Prompt: *"Act as a marketing strategist. Develop a marketing strategy for a nonfiction book on digital detox."*

This helps you create a focused and effective marketing plan.

Step 10: Gather and implement feedback

Continuously gathering feedback from your audience helps improve your book and keeps it aligned with their evolving needs. Implementing feedback demonstrates that you value your readers' opinions, which can build loyalty and enhance the quality of your work.

- Example Prompt: *"Act as a feedback specialist. Suggest ways to gather and implement reader feedback for a book on sustainable living."*

Implementing this feedback ensures your book remains relevant and valuable.

By following these detailed steps and using ChatGPT for customer profiling and market research, you can create a comprehensive, accurate, and reliable understanding of your audience and the market. This strategic approach ensures that your book resonates with readers, meets their needs, and stands out in the competitive market of nonfiction writing.

Illustrative Examples

Example 1: Market research and customer profile analysis for a book on "weight loss through plant-based diets"

- Steps 1-3: Define the niche market, pose guiding questions, and seek information.
    - Example Prompt: *"Act as a nutrition expert. What are the most popular and effective plant-based diets currently?"* and *"What are the benefits of losing weight through a plant-based diet?"*
- Steps 4-5: Analyze, evaluate data, and identify the target audience.
    - Example Prompt: *"Act as a market researcher. Summarize the target audience for a book on weight loss through plant-based diets."*

Example 2: Market research and customer profile analysis for a book on "remote working skills"

- Steps 1-3: Define the niche market, pose guiding questions, and seek information.

  - Example Prompt: *"Act as a business consultant. What are the current trends in remote working, and what methods are popular?"*

- Steps 4-5: Analyze, evaluate data, and identify the target audience.

  - Example Prompt: *"Act as a market analyst. Identify the target audience for a book on remote working skills."*

Example 3: Market research and customer profile analysis for a book on "english learning for adults"

- Steps 1-3: Define the niche market, pose guiding questions, and seek information.

  - Example Prompt: *"Act as a language expert. What are the effective and unique methods for learning English currently?"*

- Steps 4-5: Analyze, evaluate data, and identify the target audience.

  - Example Prompt: *"Act as a market researcher. Who is the target audience for a book on learning English through spatial memory techniques?"*

Example 4: Market research and customer profile analysis for a book on "online business for beginners"

- Steps 1-3: Define the niche market, pose guiding questions, and seek information.

  - Example Prompt: *"Act as a business strategist. What are the popular business models for online businesses, and what are their benefits?"*

- Steps 4-5: Analyze, evaluate data, and identify the target audience.

  - Example Prompt: *"Act as a market analyst. Describe the target audience for an eBook on starting an online business."*

ChatGPT for market research and customer profile analysis will help you better understand the needs and desires of your target customers, thereby creating products that meet their requirements.

By following these outlined steps and applying the examples of ChatGPT prompts, you will effectively use ChatGPT to support your book writing process, from exploring trends and styles to finalizing and publishing your work. This strategic approach ensures that your book is not only well-written but also aligns with current market trends and appeals to your target audience.

Chapter 14. Writing Content with ChatGPT

In the journey of writing a book, crafting engaging and high-quality content is the heart of the process. With advancements in artificial intelligence, particularly ChatGPT, authors now have a powerful tool to aid in generating, refining, and perfecting their book's content.

This chapter will guide you through the practical steps of leveraging ChatGPT to write your book, from ideation to final drafts.

Step 1: Brainstorming ideas

The first step in writing a book is brainstorming ideas. ChatGPT can help you generate a wide range of concepts and themes based on your initial thoughts, providing a foundation to build your content. This step is crucial because it sets the direction and scope of your book, ensuring you have a well-defined starting point. By exploring various themes, you can identify the most compelling and relevant topics that will resonate with your target audience.

- Example Prompt: *"Act as a creative writer. Generate a list of unique themes for a nonfiction book about sustainable living. Include a brief description for each theme."*

This helps you explore diverse themes that can serve as the backbone of your book.

Step 2: Structuring your book

A well-structured book ensures that your content flows logically and keeps readers engaged. ChatGPT can assist in outlining the main sections and chapters of your book, providing a clear roadmap for your writing. Structuring your book is essential for maintaining coherence and ensuring that each part of your book builds upon the previous sections. This step allows you to organize your thoughts and materials systematically, making the writing process more efficient and effective.

- Example Prompt: *"Act as a book editor. Create a detailed outline for a nonfiction book on the zero waste lifestyle. Include key points and subtopics for each chapter."*

This provides a comprehensive framework for your book, ensuring each chapter builds on the last.

Step 3: Writing content for each chapter

With a clear outline, you can start writing the content for each chapter. ChatGPT can generate initial drafts, provide detailed information, and enhance your writing with examples and anecdotes. This step is vital for transforming your ideas and structure into actual content. By leveraging ChatGPT, you can produce high-quality drafts quickly, ensuring that your book's narrative is engaging and informative from the start.

- Example Prompt: *"Act as a nonfiction writer. Write an introduction for the chapter on reducing waste at home. Include an engaging anecdote and a summary of what the chapter will cover."*

This draft serves as a solid starting point for your chapter.

Step 4: Enhancing and refining content

Refining your content is essential for clarity, engagement, and coherence. ChatGPT can help edit and enhance your writing by suggesting improvements and ensuring your message is clear. This step involves revising your drafts to improve their readability, flow, and overall quality. By refining your content, you ensure that your book effectively communicates its ideas and keeps readers engaged throughout.

- Example Prompt: *"Act as an editor. Improve the clarity and engagement of this paragraph: 'Recycling is important because it reduces waste and conserves natural resources. It also decreases pollution and saves energy.' Expand on the benefits and include an example."*

Step 5: Integrating examples and case studies

Real-world examples and case studies enhance your content's credibility and relatability. ChatGPT can provide detailed examples that illustrate key points and make your content more compelling. This step involves incorporating relevant examples and case studies to support your arguments and provide practical insights. By doing so, you make your book more persuasive and relatable to readers.

- Example Prompt: *"Act as a sustainability expert. Provide a detailed case study of a business successfully implementing zero-waste practices. Highlight their strategies and outcomes."*

Step 6: Developing supporting visuals

Visual aids such as charts, graphs, and infographics enhance the readability and understanding of your content. ChatGPT can suggest ideas for visuals that complement your text. This step involves creating visual elements that help convey complex information in an easily digestible format. Visual aids can make your book more engaging and help readers better understand key concepts.

- Example Prompt: *"Act as a visual content creator. Suggest visual aids for a chapter on the benefits of a plant-based diet. Include descriptions of each visual."*

Step 7: Ensuring accuracy and validity

Ensuring the accuracy of your content is critical for building trust with your readers. ChatGPT can help cross-check facts and provide references to reliable sources. This step involves verifying the information you present to ensure it is accurate, up-to-date, and credible. By doing so, you establish your book as a trustworthy source of information.

- Example Prompt: *"Act as a fact-checker. Verify the accuracy of this statement: 'Plastic takes up to 1000 years to decompose in landfills.' Provide sources for verification."*

This verification ensures your content is accurate and trustworthy.

Step 8: Finalizing and polishing the manuscript

The final step involves polishing your manuscript to ensure it is ready for publication. ChatGPT can assist with final edits, proofreading, and formatting to ensure a professional finish. This step is crucial for refining your book's content and presentation, making it polished and professional. Finalizing the manuscript ensures that your book meets the highest standards of quality and is ready for publication.

- Example Prompt: *"Act as a proofreader. Review this chapter for grammatical errors, clarity, and formatting consistency. Provide a list of suggested corrections and improvements."*

By following these detailed steps and using ChatGPT effectively, you can create a comprehensive, accurate, and engaging nonfiction book. This strategic approach ensures that your book not only meets the high standards of content quality but also resonates with your readers, helping you achieve success in your writing journey.

Illustrative Examples

Example 1: Writing "Time management for remote workers"

Step 1-2: Brainstorming ideas and structuring your book

- Example Prompt: *"Act as a productivity consultant. Identify the key challenges remote workers face in managing their time effectively. Generate a list of innovative strategies to address these challenges."*

Step 3-4: Writing and refining content

- Example Prompt: *"Act as a nonfiction writer. Draft an engaging introduction for a chapter on overcoming time management pitfalls for remote workers. Include a real-life scenario and a preview of the solutions discussed in the chapter. Then, as an editor, revise this paragraph to enhance its clarity and engagement: 'Remote workers often struggle with time management due to a lack of structure. Implementing routines can significantly improve productivity.' Expand on the benefits and provide a concrete example."*

Step 5-6: Integrating examples, case studies, and supporting visuals

- Example Prompt: *"Act as a case study analyst. Provide a detailed example of a remote worker who successfully improved their time management skills. Describe the strategies they used and the outcomes achieved. Then, as a graphic designer, create visual concepts for a chapter on time management tools for remote workers. Describe each visual and its purpose, such as charts, infographics, and checklists."*

Step 7-8: Ensuring accuracy and validity, finalizing the manuscript

- Example Prompt: *"Act as a fact-checker. Validate the accuracy of this statement: 'Using dedicated time management apps can increase remote worker productivity by 25%.' Find reliable sources to support this claim. Then, as a copyeditor, review this chapter for coherence, grammatical accuracy, and stylistic consistency. Suggest improvements to enhance readability and flow."*

Example 2: Writing "The science of mindfulness for busy professionals"

Step 1-2: Brainstorming ideas and structuring your book

- Example Prompt: *"Act as a wellness consultant. Identify the primary stressors for busy professionals and brainstorm mindfulness techniques tailored to their needs. Outline a potential chapter structure for the book."*

Step 3-4: Writing and refining content

- Example Prompt: *"Act as a nonfiction writer. Compose an engaging introduction for a chapter on the benefits of mindfulness in reducing workplace stress. Include an anecdote about a professional who improved their well-being through mindfulness. Then, as an editor, refine this paragraph for clarity and engagement: 'Mindfulness practices can help busy professionals manage stress. Techniques like deep breathing and meditation promote relaxation and focus.' Expand on the techniques and provide a practical example."*

Step 5-6: Integrating examples, case studies, and supporting visuals

- Example Prompt: *"Act as a case study writer. Detail the story of a professional who successfully incorporated mindfulness into their daily routine. Highlight the specific techniques used and the positive outcomes experienced. Then, as an infographic designer, create visual representations for a chapter on mindfulness exercises for busy professionals. Include descriptions of each visual, such as step-by-step guides and benefits charts."*

Step 7-8: Ensuring accuracy and validity, finalizing the manuscript

- Example Prompt: *"Act as a research analyst. Verify the accuracy of this statement: 'Regular mindfulness practice can reduce stress levels by up to 40%.' Provide supporting evidence from recent studies. Then, as a proofreader, review this chapter for grammatical accuracy, clarity, and consistency. Offer suggestions for enhancing the overall readability and impact."*

By following these steps and utilizing ChatGPT effectively, you can create comprehensive, accurate, and engaging nonfiction books. This structured approach ensures that your books not only meet high standards of content quality but also resonate with your readers, helping you achieve success in your writing journey.

Chapter 15. Competitors & Market Research

Creating a best-selling book involves more than just writing talent; it requires in-depth knowledge of the subject and effective research of your competitors. With advancements in artificial intelligence, ChatGPT has become a valuable tool for conducting competitive research before you begin writing your book.

This chapter will guide you on how to leverage ChatGPT to gather information about your competitors, analyze data, and create high-quality content. Follow these steps to maximize ChatGPT's capabilities in researching competitors and crafting an engaging book.

Step 1: Identify your competitors

Identifying your competitors is the foundation of competitive research. Understanding who your competitors are and what they offer allows you to position your book uniquely in the market. This step ensures that you are aware of the current landscape, which is crucial for differentiating your content and finding gaps in the market that you can fill with your unique insights.

- Example Prompt: *"Act as a market researcher with expertise in the publishing industry. Identify the top 10 best-selling books on productivity from the past three years, and highlight any emerging trends or common themes among these titles. Focus on both their market performance and content strategies."*
- Example Prompt:*"Act as a market analyst specializing in self-help literature. Provide a detailed analysis of the leading authors in the self-help genre, including their most successful works, writing styles, and key marketing strategies that contributed to their popularity."*

Step 2: Analyze competitors' content

Analyzing your competitors' content helps you understand their strengths and weaknesses. This insight is vital for identifying what works well and what doesn't in the market. By evaluating reviews, you can discern common themes and reader preferences, which will guide you in enhancing your own book to meet and exceed market expectations.

- Example Prompt: *"Act as a literary critic and market analyst. Conduct a detailed review analysis of James Clear's 'Atomic Habits,' focusing on its strengths, weaknesses, and reader feedback patterns. Identify what aspects of the book resonate most with readers and which areas received criticism."*

Step 3: Discover unique angles for your content

Finding unique angles for your content is essential for standing out in a crowded market. This step involves brainstorming innovative ideas and perspectives that differentiate your book from others. By identifying unique selling points, you ensure that your content is fresh, engaging, and has a distinctive voice that attracts readers.

- Example Prompt: *"Act as a creative strategist with a focus on nonfiction. Brainstorm innovative angles for a productivity book that combines psychology and technology, providing ideas that will set it apart from current bestsellers in the market. Suggest how these angles could appeal to a broad audience while addressing specific niches."*

Step 4: Develop engaging content

Developing engaging content is about translating your research into compelling writing that captures and retains reader interest. This step focuses on crafting content that is not only informative but also enjoyable to read. Utilizing ChatGPT for specific sections can help refine your language, enhance clarity, and add depth to your narrative.

- Example Prompt: *"Act as a professional writer and content strategist. How can I draft a captivating introduction for a book on productivity that hooks the reader from the first sentence? The introduction should set the stage by addressing common productivity challenges and promising actionable solutions."*
- Example Prompt: *"Act as a subject matter expert in productivity techniques. Provide engaging and relatable examples to illustrate the Pomodoro Technique, ensuring the explanations are clear, motivational, and accessible to readers of all backgrounds."*

Step 5: Review and refine

Reviewing and refining your content is crucial for ensuring it is polished and professional. This step involves using ChatGPT to critique your work, suggesting improvements in structure, coherence, and readability. Regular review cycles help to identify areas of improvement and ensure that your book maintains high standards of quality.

- Example Prompt: *"Act as an experienced editor specializing in nonfiction. Review the following content from my book on productivity, focusing on structure, coherence, and readability. Provide specific suggestions for improvement, including how to enhance clarity and engagement. Here is the content: [Insert content]"*

Step 6: Plan Your marketing strategy

Planning an effective marketing strategy is essential for maximizing your book's reach and sales. This step involves using ChatGPT to devise a comprehensive marketing plan that includes online promotion, social media strategies, and potential partnerships. A well-thought-out marketing strategy ensures that your book gains the visibility it deserves and reaches its target audience.

- Example Prompt: *"Act as a marketing consultant with experience in the publishing industry. Develop a comprehensive marketing strategy for a book on productivity. Include targeted online promotion tactics, social media engagement strategies, and potential partnerships or collaborations that could boost visibility and sales. The strategy should focus on reaching both general readers and specific niches interested in productivity."*

Illustrative Examples:

Example 1: Writing a book on public speaking

Steps 1-2: Identify competitors and analyze competitors' content

- Example Prompt: *"Act as a market researcher with a focus on nonfiction books. Identify the top five best-selling books on public speaking from the past two years. Include details on their authors, publication dates, and any noteworthy marketing strategies that contributed to their success."*
- Example Prompt: *"Act as a literary critic. Conduct a detailed analysis of the reviews for 'Speak Like a Pro' by Jane Doe. Identify common themes in reader feedback, focusing on both the strengths and areas where the book could be improved."*

Steps 3-4: Discover unique angles and develop engaging content

- Example Prompt: *"Act as a creative strategist specializing in self-help books. Propose three innovative approaches to writing about public speaking that would differentiate my book from current bestsellers. Consider angles that address underexplored topics or new audience segments."*
- Example Prompt: *"Act as a professional writer with experience in crafting nonfiction introductions. Help me write a captivating and engaging introduction for a book on public speaking that immediately draws in readers and sets the tone for the rest of the book."*

Steps 5-6: Review and refine and plan your marketing strategy

- Example Prompt: *"Act as an experienced book editor. Critique my chapter on overcoming stage fright, focusing on structure, clarity, and reader engagement. Provide specific suggestions for improvement. Here is my chapter: [Insert chapter]"*
- Example Prompt: *"Act as a marketing consultant with expertise in book promotions. Recommend the most effective marketing strategies for a book on public speaking, considering both online and offline channels. Include ideas for social media campaigns, partnerships, and events."*

Example 2: Writing a book on mindfulness

Steps 1-2: Identify competitors and analyze competitors' content

- Example Prompt: *"Act as a market researcher with expertise in the wellness and mindfulness sector. Identify the top five best-selling books on mindfulness from the last 18 months. Include details on their key selling points and any promotional strategies that helped them stand out."*
- Example Prompt: *"Act as a literary critic. Analyze the reviews for 'The Mindful Path' by John Smith and identify its"Act as a literary critic specializing in wellness literature. Analyze the reviews for 'The Mindful Path' by John Smith. Summarize the book's strengths and weaknesses based on reader feedback, and suggest how these insights could inform my writing." strengths and weaknesses."*

Steps 3-4: Discover unique angles and develop engaging content

- Example Prompt: *"Act as a creative strategist focused on wellness content. Suggest three innovative ideas for writing about mindfulness that could attract a modern audience. Consider integrating contemporary issues or blending mindfulness with other disciplines."*

- Example Prompt: *"Act as a professional writer with a background in wellness. Help me craft a compelling and relatable introduction for a book on mindfulness, ensuring it resonates with readers and sets a reflective tone for the rest of the content."*

Steps 5-6: Review and refine and plan your marketing strategy

- Example Prompt: *"Act as an experienced editor. Review my section on mindfulness meditation techniques, focusing on clarity, coherence, and engagement. Provide constructive feedback to enhance the section's readability and effectiveness. Here is my section: [Insert section]"*
- Example Prompt: *"Act as a marketing consultant with a specialization in wellness books. Suggest effective marketing strategies for promoting a mindfulness book, including online advertising, influencer partnerships, and community engagement activities."*

Chapter 16. Writing Nonfiction with ChatGPT

ChatGPT is an invaluable tool for authors, particularly when it comes to writing nonfiction books. By creating precise prompts that outline your book's topic and objectives, you can leverage ChatGPT to generate titles, outlines, and even complete chapters. This chapter will guide you through the process of using ChatGPT effectively, using health and wellness as an example theme.

The purpose of this chapter is to demonstrate how ChatGPT can be utilized throughout the book writing process, from generating outlines to writing full chapters.

Step 1: Generate an outline for your book

Creating a structured outline is the first step in writing a nonfiction book, serving as a roadmap that guides you through the content and ensures a logical flow of information. By organizing your thoughts and ideas systematically, an outline makes the writing process more efficient and coherent. It helps identify the main topics and subtopics, ensuring no important aspect is overlooked and allowing you to manage the writing process effectively.

- Example Prompt: *"Act as a wellness expert. Please create an outline for a nonfiction book on health and wellness. The book should be approximately 200 pages and include chapters on nutrition, exercise, and mental health."*

Step 2: Generate options for titles and subtitles

Crafting a compelling title and subtitle is crucial for attracting readers, as a well-chosen title conveys the essence of your book and piques the interest of your target audience. Generating multiple title and subtitle options allows you to explore different angles and approaches, helping you identify the most impactful and appealing title that aligns with your book's content and audience. This process ensures your book stands out in the market and effectively captures the attention of potential readers

- Example Prompt: *"Act as a book marketing specialist. Please suggest five different title and subtitle options for a book about health and wellness. The book includes chapters on nutrition, exercise, and mental health."*

Step 3: Write complete chapters

Once you have your outline and titles, the next step is writing the chapters. ChatGPT can assist by providing detailed content for each chapter, streamlining the writing process and generating high-quality content efficiently. Using ChatGPT for writing complete chapters ensures each chapter is well-developed, informative, and engaging, making the entire book cohesive and compelling for readers. This approach saves time and maintains a consistent tone and style throughout your work.

- Example Prompt: *"Act as an experienced nonfiction author. Please write Chapter 2, titled 'Nutrition: Fueling Your Body for Optimal Health,' of a nonfiction book called 'The Wellness Guide: Achieving Optimal Health through Nutrition, Exercise, and Mental Well-Being'. This chapter should discuss the importance of a balanced diet, understanding macronutrients and micronutrients, debunking common dietary myths, and providing practical tips for meal planning and hydration. The chapter should be engaging, informative, and approximately 1,500 words long."*

Step 4: Review and refine content

Reviewing and refining your content is crucial to ensure clarity, coherence, and overall quality. ChatGPT can provide constructive feedback and suggestions for improvement, helping to enhance the readability and professionalism of your writing. This step helps identify and rectify any inconsistencies, errors, or areas that require further development, ensuring your book is polished and engaging for readers.

- Example Prompt: *"Act as an editor. Can you critique my chapter on nutrition and suggest improvements? Here is my chapter: [Insert chapter]"*

Step 5: Plan your marketing strategy

A well-planned marketing strategy is essential for the success of your book. ChatGPT can help you develop effective marketing plans to reach your target audience and maximize sales. The purpose of planning a marketing strategy is to ensure that your book reaches its intended audience and achieves its sales goals by identifying the best channels and tactics for promotion. This step involves leveraging various marketing techniques to increase visibility and attract readers.

- Example Prompt: *"Act as a marketing consultant with expertise in the health and wellness industry. Please provide a detailed list of the most effective marketing strategies for promoting a book on health and wellness. Include approaches for social media, content marketing, influencer collaborations, email campaigns, and any other relevant tactics to maximize reach and engagement."*

Illustrative Examples

Example 1: Writing a book on sustainable business practices

Step 1: Generate an outline for your book

- Example Prompt: *"Act as a sustainability expert. Please create an outline for a nonfiction book on sustainable business practices. The book should be approximately 200 pages and include chapters on sustainable supply chains, eco-friendly product design, and corporate social responsibility."*

Step 2: Generate options for titles and subtitles

- Example Prompt: *"Act as a book marketing specialist. Please suggest five different title and subtitle options for a book about sustainable business practices. The book includes chapters on sustainable supply chains, eco-friendly product design, and corporate social responsibility."*

Step 3: Write complete chapters

- Example Prompt: *"Act as an experienced nonfiction author. Please write Chapter 3, titled 'Sustainable Supply Chains: Reducing Your Carbon Footprint,' of a nonfiction book called 'Green Business: Strategies for Sustainable Success'. This chapter should discuss the importance of sustainable sourcing, strategies for reducing carbon footprint in supply chains, and case studies of successful sustainable supply chains. The chapter should be engaging, informative, and approximately 1,500 words long."*

Step 4: Review and refine content

- Example Prompt: *"Act as an editor. Can you critique my chapter on sustainable supply chains and suggest improvements? Here is my chapter: [Insert chapter]"*

Step 5: Plan Your marketing strategy

- Example Prompt: *"Act as a marketing consultant with expertise in the sustainability industry. Please provide a detailed list of the most effective marketing strategies for promoting a book on sustainable business practices. Include approaches for social media, content marketing, influencer collaborations, email campaigns, and any other relevant tactics to maximize reach and engagement."*

Example 2: Writing a book on remote work strategies

Step 1: Generate an outline for your book

- Example Prompt: *"Act as a remote work expert. Please create an outline for a nonfiction book on remote work strategies. The book should be approximately 200 pages and include chapters on productivity, communication, and work-life balance."*

Step 2: Generate Options for titles and subtitles

- Example Prompt: *"Act as a book marketing specialist. Please suggest five different title and subtitle options for a book about remote work strategies. The book includes chapters on productivity, communication, and work-life balance."*

Step 3: Write complete chapters

- Example Prompt: *"Act as an experienced nonfiction author. Please write Chapter 4, titled 'Productivity: Tools and Strategies for Remote Work,' of a nonfiction book called 'Remote Work Revolution: Mastering Productivity, Communication, and Work-Life Balance'. This chapter should discuss tools and technologies for remote work, time management strategies, setting up an effective home office, and overcoming productivity challenges. The chapter should be engaging, informative, and approximately 1,500 words long."*

Step 4: Review and refine content

- Example Prompt: *"Act as an editor. Can you critique my chapter on remote work productivity and suggest improvements? Here is my chapter: [Insert chapter]"*

Step 5: Plan Your marketing strategy

- Example Prompt: *"Act as a marketing consultant with expertise in the remote work industry. Please provide a detailed list of the most effective marketing strategies for promoting a book on remote work strategies. Include approaches for social media, content marketing, influencer collaborations, email campaigns, and any other relevant tactics to maximize reach and engagement."*

Chapter 17. Clickbait Titles

The title of your book can make or break its success. An engaging, attention-grabbing title is crucial for drawing readers in and sparking their curiosity. This chapter will walk you through how to effectively use ChatGPT to craft compelling, clickbait titles that ensure your book stands out in a crowded market.

By mastering these techniques, you'll not only capture the interest of potential readers but also motivate them to dive deeper into your content. With the right title, you can significantly boost your book's visibility and appeal.

Step 1: Define your goal and audience

Understanding your goal and audience is crucial for tailoring your title to meet their interests and needs. It ensures that your book appeals to the right readers and effectively communicates its value proposition. This foundational step sets the direction for your entire project, helping to align your content with the expectations and preferences of your target market. By defining your audience and goals, you can craft a title that not only attracts attention but also resonates deeply with potential readers.

Example:

- Goal: To teach beginners how to invest in cryptocurrency.
- Audience: New investors looking to understand the basics of cryptocurrency.

Step 2: Research engaging keywords and phrases

Researching keywords helps in understanding what potential readers are searching for. This step ensures your title contains terms that increase visibility and attract clicks. Incorporating well-researched keywords into your title enhances its SEO value, making your book easier to find in search results. Additionally, it helps you tap into the language and phrases that resonate most with your audience, increasing the likelihood of capturing their interest and driving engagement.

Example:

- Keywords: cryptocurrency, investment, get rich, secrets, beginners.

Step 3: Use ChatGPT to generate titles

Combine the information from Steps 1 and 2 into a prompt for ChatGPT. This will help generate a variety of potential titles.

Using ChatGPT to generate titles allows for creative brainstorming and exploration of different angles. It ensures you have multiple options to choose from, increasing the chances of finding a highly effective title. This process leverages the AI's ability to produce diverse and innovative suggestions that you might not have considered, broadening your creative horizons and enhancing the appeal of your final title selection.

- Example Prompt: *"Act as a marketing expert and create five engaging, attention-grabbing, and clickbait titles for a book on how beginners can get rich from cryptocurrency investments. Use the keywords: cryptocurrency, investment, get rich, secrets, beginners."*

Step 4: Evaluate and choose the best title

Evaluating and choosing the best title ensures that the final choice accurately reflects your book's content and appeals to your target audience. This step is crucial for maximizing the title's impact and effectiveness. By carefully assessing each option, you can identify the title that not only draws attention but also promises the value your book delivers, encouraging potential readers to click and explore further.

- Prompt Example: *"Act as a literary agent. Evaluate the following list of potential titles for a book about cryptocurrency investments for beginners and choose the one that best reflects the book's content and appeals to the target audience. Provide reasons for your selection. Here are the titles: [Insert title 1], [Insert title 2] and [Insert title 3]"*

Step 5: Refine the title

Refining the title enhances its appeal and ensures it is clear, concise, and compelling. This step is important for making a strong first impression on potential readers. Polishing your title ensures it is free from ambiguity and effectively conveys the essence of your book, thereby increasing its attractiveness and click-through potential. A refined title helps to build trust and sets the right expectations for your audience.

- Prompt Example: *"Act as a seasoned book editor. Refine the title 'Cryptocurrency Secrets: How Beginners Can Get Rich Quick' to make it more compelling, clear, and professional. Ensure it effectively conveys the book's value and appeals to the target audience."*

Illustrative Examples

Example 1: Creating a title for a book on "English Learning for Working Professionals"

Step 1: Define your goal and audience

- Goal: Enhance English skills for career advancement.
- Audience: Working professionals.

Step 2: Research engaging keywords and phrases

- Keywords: English, working professionals, enhance skills, career advancement.

Step 3: Use ChatGPT to generate titles

- Improved Prompt: *"Act as a language learning expert and create five engaging, attention-grabbing, and clickbait titles for an book on enhancing English skills for working professionals. Use the keywords: English, working professionals, enhance skills, career advancement."*

Step 4: Evaluate and choose the best title

- Selected Title: "Advance Your Career with English: Secret Skills Enhancement for Working Professionals"

Step 5: Refine the title

- Refined title: "Advance Your Career with English: Essential Skills Enhancement for Working Professionals"

Example 2: Creating a title for an book on "Budget Backpacking"

Step 1: Define your goal and audience

- Goal: Share budget backpacking experiences.
- Audience: Young travelers.

Step 2: Research engaging keywords and phrases

- Keywords: backpacking, budget, experiences, young travelers.

Step 3: Use ChatGPT to generate titles

- Example Prompt: *"Act as a travel blogger and create five engaging, attention-grabbing, and clickbait titles for a book sharing experiences on budget backpacking for young travelers. Use the keywords: backpacking, budget, experiences, young travelers."*

Step 4: Evaluate and choose the best title

- Selected title: "Ultimate Budget Backpacking: Essential Guide for Young Adventurers!"

Step 5: Refine the title

- Refined title: "Ultimate Budget Backpacking: A Guide for Young Adventurers"

Creating a compelling title is crucial for attracting readers to your eBook. By defining your goal and audience, researching engaging keywords, using ChatGPT to generate titles, and refining your chosen title, you can craft a title that captures attention and drives clicks. Embrace these strategies to enhance your eBook's success and reach a wider audience.

Chapter 18. Table of Contents Creation

Developing a compelling table of contents is crucial for capturing readers' interest and providing a clear roadmap through your book. In this chapter, you'll learn how to effectively use ChatGPT to create a detailed and professional table of contents that not only stands out but also guides your readers seamlessly through your content.

By mastering these techniques, you can ensure your table of contents is both engaging and functional.

Step 1: Understand the purpose and target audience

Understanding your book's purpose and target audience ensures that your content is relevant and engaging. By knowing who your readers are and what they need, you can tailor your topics to address their specific challenges and goals effectively. This foundational step helps you stay focused and organized throughout the writing process, ultimately leading to a more cohesive and impactful book.

- Example Prompt: *"Act as a market research analyst. Help me understand the purpose and target audience for a book about healthy living. Define the primary goals the book should achieve and describe the characteristics and needs of the target readers to ensure the content is relevant and engaging."*

Step 2: Compile and arrange content

Compiling and arranging content helps in organizing your thoughts systematically. This step ensures that your book flows logically and covers all necessary aspects comprehensively. By structuring your content effectively, you make it easier for readers to follow along and grasp the key messages, enhancing their overall reading experience and satisfaction.

- Example Prompt: *"Act as an experienced nonfiction author. Help me compile and arrange content for a book about healthy living. Outline the main chapters and subtopics in a logical order to ensure the book flows smoothly and comprehensively covers all necessary aspects."*

Step 3: Use ChatGPT to break down titles into smaller sections

Breaking down titles into smaller sections makes your content more digestible for readers. This step ensures that each topic is covered in detail, enhancing the overall readability and engagement of your book. It also helps in highlighting key points clearly, allowing readers to easily navigate and absorb the information.

- Example Prompt: *"Act as a nonfiction book editor. Help me break down the main titles of my book on healthy living into smaller sections. Subdivide each chapter into more manageable subtopics and create engaging subheadings for these sections to enhance readability and engagement."*

Step 4: Optimize titles

Optimizing titles helps in attracting readers' attention. Engaging titles can significantly increase the appeal of your book, making readers more likely to delve into your content. Well-crafted titles not only intrigue readers but also convey the essence of each section, enhancing their overall interest and engagement.

- Example Prompt: *"Act as a book marketing expert. Help me optimize the titles of each chapter in my healthy living book to make them more engaging and appealing. Ensure the titles are captivating and accurately convey the essence of each section."*

Step 5: Add clickbait keywords

Adding clickbait keywords ensures that your titles are compelling and attractive. This step helps in drawing readers in and keeping them engaged with your book. By using powerful and appealing keywords, you can enhance the marketability of your book and increase its visibility in search results and recommendations.

- Example Prompt: *"Act as an SEO specialist. Suggest clickbait keywords to enhance the titles of each chapter in my healthy living book, making them more compelling and attractive to readers. Ensure the keywords are engaging and improve the book's visibility in search results."*

Step 6: Review and edit titles

Reviewing and refining titles ensures that they are clear, concise, and impactful. This step helps in enhancing the professionalism and readability of your table of contents. By meticulously editing your titles, you ensure they effectively communicate the value of your content and attract your target audience.

- Example Prompt: *"Act as a professional editor. Review and refine the titles in my healthy living book's table of contents. Ensure that each title is clear, concise, and impactful, effectively communicating the value of the content and attracting my target audience."*

Step 7: Ensure consistency

Ensuring consistency in language and style makes your table of contents professional and easy to navigate. This step helps in providing a seamless reading experience for your audience. Consistency in presentation not only enhances the aesthetic appeal of your book but also reinforces your credibility as an author.

- Example Prompt: *"Act as a style consultant. Review the language and style of my healthy living book's table of contents. Ensure that it maintains consistency in terms of tone, vocabulary, and formatting, providing a seamless and professional reading experience for my audience. Here is the table of contents: [Insert the table of contents]"*

Illustrative Examples

Example 1: Writing a book on gardening

Step 1: Understand the purpose and target audience

- Example Prompt: *"Act as a market research analyst. Help me understand the purpose and target audience for a book about organic gardening. Define the primary goals the book should achieve and describe the characteristics and needs of the target readers to ensure the content is relevant and engaging."*

Step 2: Compile and arrange content

- Example Prompt: *"Act as an experienced nonfiction author. Help me compile and arrange content for a book about organic gardening. Outline the main chapters and subtopics in a logical order to ensure the book flows smoothly and comprehensively covers all necessary aspects."*

Step 3: Use ChatGPT to break down titles into smaller sections

- Example Prompt: *"Act as a nonfiction book editor. Help me break down the main titles of my book on organic gardening into smaller sections. Subdivide each chapter into more manageable subtopics and create engaging subheadings for these sections to enhance readability and engagement."*

Step 4: Optimize Titles

- Example Prompt: *"Act as a book marketing expert. Help me optimize the titles of each chapter in my organic gardening book to make them more engaging and appealing. Ensure the titles are captivating and accurately convey the essence of each section."*

Step 5: Add clickbait keywords

- Example Prompt: *"Act as an SEO specialist. Suggest clickbait keywords to enhance the titles of each chapter in my organic gardening book, making them more compelling and attractive to readers. Ensure the keywords are engaging and improve the book's visibility in search results."*

Step 6: Review and Edit Titles

- Example Prompt: *"Act as a professional editor. Review and refine the titles in my organic gardening book's table of contents. Ensure that each title is clear, concise, and impactful, effectively communicating the value of the content and attracting my target audience."*

Step 7: Ensure Consistency

- Example Prompt: *"Act as a style consultant. Review the language and style of my organic gardening book's table of contents. Ensure that it maintains consistency in terms of tone, vocabulary, and formatting, providing a seamless and professional reading experience for my audience. Here is the table of contents: [Insert the table of contents]"*

Example 2: Writing a book on personal finance

Step 1: Understand the purpose and target audience

- Example Prompt: *"Act as a market research analyst. Help me understand the purpose and target audience for a book about personal finance. Define the primary goals the book should achieve and describe the characteristics and needs of the target readers to ensure the content is relevant and engaging."*

Step 2: Compile and arrange content

- Example Prompt: *"Act as an experienced nonfiction author. Help me compile and arrange content for a book about personal finance. Outline the main chapters and subtopics in a logical order to ensure the book flows smoothly and comprehensively covers all necessary aspects."*

Step 3: Use ChatGPT to break down titles into smaller sections

- Example Prompt: *"Act as a nonfiction book editor. Help me break down the main titles of my book on personal finance into smaller sections. Subdivide each chapter into more manageable subtopics and create engaging subheadings for these sections to enhance readability and engagement."*

Step 4: Optimize titles

- Example Prompt: *"Act as a book marketing expert. Help me optimize the titles of each chapter in my personal finance book to make them more engaging and appealing. Ensure the titles are captivating and accurately convey the essence of each section."*

Step 5: Add clickbait keywords

- Example Prompt: *"Act as an SEO specialist. Suggest clickbait keywords to enhance the titles of each chapter in my personal finance book, making them more compelling and attractive to readers. Ensure the keywords are engaging and improve the book's visibility in search results."*

Step 6: Review and edit titles

- Example Prompt: *"Act as a professional editor. Review and refine the titles in my personal finance book's table of contents. Ensure that each title is clear, concise, and impactful, effectively communicating the value of the content and attracting my target audience."*

Step 7: Ensure Consistency

- Example Prompt: *"Act as a style consultant. Review the language and style of my personal finance book's table of contents. Ensure that it maintains consistency in terms of tone, vocabulary, and formatting, providing a seamless and professional reading experience for my audience. Here is the table of contents: [Insert the table of contents]"*

By following these detailed steps and utilizing the illustrative examples, you can beffectively use ChatGPT to create engaging, clickbait titles for your ook. This approach not only enhances the attractiveness of your content but also ensures it is relevant, organized, and optimized for your target audience.

Chapter 19. Creating Engaging Content

Harness the potential of ChatGPT to create engaging and high-quality content for your book. In this chapter, you'll discover a step-by-step guide to leveraging ChatGPT for efficient content creation, ensuring that your writing is both captivating and well-organized.

By following these strategies, you can streamline your writing process, save time, and produce content that resonates with your audience.

Step 1: Identify topics and subtopics

This step helps you establish a clear roadmap for your book, ensuring that you cover all relevant areas comprehensively. It also helps in structuring your thoughts systematically, making the writing process more manageable and efficient. Additionally, it allows you to identify gaps in your knowledge early, giving you time to research and fill these gaps before you start writing.

- Example Prompt: *"Act as a fitness expert specializing in holistic wellness. Help me brainstorm 10 key topics and relevant subtopics for a book on 'Holistic Wellness,' ensuring the content covers physical, mental, and emotional well-being comprehensively."*

Step 2: Create questions or prompts

Creating questions or prompts ensures that the content generated is focused and detailed. It helps you delve deeper into each subtopic, providing valuable information to your readers. Furthermore, it keeps the writing process organized and ensures that you maintain a consistent and comprehensive approach to each section of your book.

- Example Prompt: *"Act as a fitness expert with a focus on holistic health. Develop five in-depth and thought-provoking questions to explore the essential principles of holistic wellness, aiming to engage readers and encourage deeper reflection."*

Step 3: Use ChatGPT to generate content

Utilizing ChatGPT to generate content allows you to produce high-quality material efficiently. It ensures that your content is well-researched, informative, and engaging, saving you time and effort in the writing process. Additionally, it allows you to experiment with different writing styles and tones, helping you find the most effective way to communicate your ideas to your audience.

- Example Prompt: *"Act as a seasoned fitness expert. Provide comprehensive and detailed answers to the five key principles of holistic wellness, ensuring each answer is informative, engaging, and applicable to readers looking to improve their well-being."*

Step 4: Review and refine the content

Reviewing and refining content ensures that it is clear, coherent, and engaging. This step helps to identify any gaps or inconsistencies and allows you to enhance the overall quality and professionalism of your writing. It also helps to ensure that your content resonates with your audience, making it more impactful and persuasive.

- Example Prompt: *"Act as a professional editor with experience in wellness literature. Review the following content on holistic wellness principles, focusing on clarity, coherence, and reader engagement. Suggest specific improvements to enhance the overall quality and impact. Here is the content: [Insert the content]"*

Step 5: Organize the content logically

Organizing content logically enhances readability and ensures a smooth flow of information. It helps readers easily navigate through the book and understand the progression of ideas. Additionally, a well-organized structure can improve the overall reader experience, making your book more enjoyable and effective.

- Example Prompt: *"Act as a content strategist with a focus on health and wellness. Help me organize these subtopics on holistic wellness into a cohesive and logical structure that guides readers naturally from one concept to the next. Here are the subtopics: [Insert the subtopics]"*

Step 6: Enhance presentation and readability

Enhancing presentation and readability ensures that your book is visually appealing and easy to read. This step helps to capture and retain readers' attention, making their reading experience more enjoyable. It also reflects your professionalism and commitment to quality, which can positively impact your readers' perception of your work.

- Example Prompt: *"Act as a book designer with experience in wellness publications. Suggest advanced formatting and design tips to enhance the readability and visual appeal of my book on holistic wellness, ensuring that it is both professional and engaging."*

Step 7: Final review and editing

The final review and editing process is crucial for ensuring that your book is polished and professional. This step helps to catch any remaining errors and ensures consistency in tone and style, resulting in a high-quality final product. It also provides an opportunity to make last-minute improvements that can enhance the overall impact of your book.

- Example Prompt: *Act as a professional editor with expertise in final manuscript preparation. Conduct a final review of my book content, highlighting areas that need refinement, ensuring consistency in tone and style, and suggesting any last-minute improvements to elevate the book's overall impact. Here is the content: [Insert the content]"*

Illustrative Examples

Step 1: Identify topics and subtopics

- Example Prompt: *"Assume the role of a digital marketing strategist. Help me brainstorm 10 key topics and 3-5 detailed subtopics for each, ensuring the book comprehensively covers modern digital marketing strategies, including SEO, social media marketing, content marketing, and email campaigns."*

Step 2: Create questions or prompts

- Example Prompt: *"Take on the role of a digital marketing consultant. Develop five thought-provoking and research-based questions that delve into the key principles of digital marketing strategies. Ensure these questions encourage deep reflection and critical thinking in readers, especially in areas like data-driven marketing and consumer behavior analysis."*

Step 3: Use ChatGPT to generate content

- Example Prompt: *"Adopt the perspective of a seasoned digital marketer. Generate detailed and engaging explanations for each of the five key principles of digital marketing strategies, ensuring the content is both informative and accessible to a general audience. Highlight practical examples where possible."*

Step 4: Review and refine the content

- Example Prompt: *"Assume the role of a senior editor specializing in digital marketing literature. Review the following content on digital marketing strategies for clarity, coherence, and reader engagement. Provide specific suggestions for improvement, focusing on enhancing the narrative flow and overall readability. Here is the content: [Insert the content]"*

Step 5: Organize the content logically

- Example Prompt: *"Take on the role of a content strategist with expertise in digital marketing. Organize the following subtopics on digital marketing strategies into a logical, reader-friendly structure. Ensure that each section builds on the previous one, creating a seamless and engaging narrative flow. Here are the subtopics: [Insert the subtopics]"*

Step 6: Enhance presentation and readability

- Example Prompt: *"Assume the role of a book designer specializing in marketing publications. Suggest advanced formatting and layout strategies that enhance both the readability and visual appeal of my book on digital marketing strategies. Focus on elements such as typography, spacing, and the use of visuals like infographics to create an inviting and accessible reader experience."*

Step 7: Final review and editing

- Example Prompt: *"Take on the role of a professional editor with a focus on final manuscript preparation in the marketing field. Conduct a thorough review of the book content, checking for consistency in tone, style, and formatting. Highlight any areas that require final revisions to ensure a polished and professional finished product. Here is the book content: [Insert the content]"*

By following these steps and using these illustrative prompts, you can effectively utilize ChatGPT to create detailed, comprehensive, and engaging content for your book. This method ensures your book is well-organized, informative, and appealing to readers, helping you achieve success in your writing endeavors.

Chapter 20. Book Descriptions

Master the art of creating book descriptions that instantly captivate readers and drive sales. In this chapter, you'll learn a six-step process for crafting compelling and irresistible descriptions with the help of ChatGPT.

By following these steps, you can ensure that your book's description not only grabs attention but also entices potential readers to explore more, ultimately boosting your book's success.

Step 1: Identify the reader's challenges and aspirations

This step helps you understand the pain points and desires of your target audience, ensuring that your book description resonates with their needs and interests. By identifying their challenges and aspirations, you can craft a description that speaks directly to them, making your book more appealing and relevant. It also sets the stage for highlighting the solutions your book offers, increasing its perceived value.

- Example Prompt: *"Adopt the perspective of a seasoned fitness coach and identify the top five challenges and aspirations of readers seeking to enhance their physical fitness. Focus on providing a nuanced understanding of these challenges across different fitness levels, from beginners to advanced practitioners."*

Step 2: Present the book's solutions

Presenting solutions directly addresses the challenges and aspirations identified in the previous step. It positions your book as a valuable resource that provides practical, actionable advice. Highlighting specific benefits helps readers see the tangible outcomes they can achieve, making them more likely to be interested in purchasing your book.

- Example Prompt: *"Assume the role of an expert fitness coach and author of 'Total Fitness Transformation.' Elaborate on the core solutions your book offers to address the most critical fitness challenges identified. Highlight how these solutions are tailored to different fitness levels and how they stand out from existing alternatives in the market."*

Step 3: Provide evidence and results

Providing evidence and results builds credibility and trust with your readers. It shows that the solutions offered in your book have been tried and tested, leading to successful outcomes. This step enhances the persuasiveness of your book description by showing potential readers that others have benefited from the advice and strategies you present.

- Example Prompt: *"As a fitness coach who has successfully implemented the strategies in 'Total Fitness Transformation,' provide three compelling case studies or testimonials that demonstrate the tangible results readers have achieved. Focus on metrics such as weight loss, muscle gain, or improved overall health."*

Step 4: Utilize persuasive language

Using persuasive language helps create an emotional connection with your readers, making them more likely to be influenced by your message. Emphasizing benefits rather than features focuses on the positive outcomes readers can achieve, which is more compelling and motivating. This step ensures your book description is not only informative but also persuasive and engaging.

- Example Prompt: *"Adopt the mindset of a seasoned copywriter and craft five persuasive, benefit-driven phrases for the book description of 'Total Fitness Transformation.' Focus on creating a sense of urgency and personal empowerment, compelling readers to take immediate action towards their fitness goals."*

Step 5: Call to action

A strong call to action directs readers on what to do next, creating a sense of urgency and encouraging immediate action. This step is crucial for converting interest into sales, ensuring that your book description not only attracts readers but also prompts them to purchase your book.

- Example Prompt: *"Channel your expertise as a marketing strategist to formulate a powerful and compelling call to action for 'Total Fitness Transformation.' Ensure the CTA drives urgency, offering incentives like limited-time discounts or exclusive access to additional resources, prompting immediate purchase decisions."*

Step 6: Integrate keywords

Integrating keywords improves the search engine optimization (SEO) of your book description, making it easier for potential readers to find your book online. This step ensures that your book appears in relevant search results, increasing its visibility and potential sales. It also helps maintain the natural flow of the description, ensuring it remains engaging and readable.

- Example Prompt: *"Assume the role of an SEO expert with a focus on book marketing. Develop a strategy for seamlessly incorporating high-impact keywords such as 'fitness,' 'weight loss,' and 'workout plans' into the book description of 'Total Fitness Transformation.' Ensure the keywords enhance SEO without disrupting the narrative flow, keeping the description engaging and naturally readable."*

Illustrative Example:

Step 1: Listing the reader's challenges and dreams

- Example Prompt: *"Act as a nutritionist who specializes in mindful eating and weight loss. Identify the top five challenges and aspirations that readers typically face, such as overcoming emotional eating or achieving sustainable weight loss. Ensure these issues resonate deeply with individuals seeking long-term lifestyle changes."*

Step 2: Solutions offered by the book

- Example Prompt: *"Act as a nutritionist and outline three innovative and practical solutions from the book 'Mindful Eating' that address common reader challenges like stress eating and portion control. Make sure these solutions are actionable and can be easily integrated into daily life."*

Step 3: Providing evidence and results

- Example Prompt: *"Act as a nutritionist and present a compelling case study or testimonial from 'Mindful Eating' that demonstrates significant results, such as a 20-pound weight loss over three months through mindful eating practices. Highlight measurable outcomes that validate the book's effectiveness."*

Step 4: Using persuasive language

- Example Prompt: *"Act as a seasoned copywriter and craft a persuasive sentence for the book description of 'Mindful Eating' that appeals to the reader's desire for a healthier lifestyle. Focus on how the book can transform their relationship with food, leading to lasting weight loss and a renewed sense of well-being."*

Step 5: Strong conclusion

- Example Prompt: *"Act as a marketing strategist and conclude the book description for 'Mindful Eating' with a powerful call-to-action that motivates readers to take control of their health today. Make sure the conclusion instills a sense of urgency and assures readers that this book is their gateway to a healthier, more mindful life."*

Crafting a compelling book description is essential for capturing the interest of potential readers and boosting your book sales. By following this six-step formula and leveraging the power of ChatGPT, you can create engaging, persuasive, and keyword-optimized descriptions that will make your book stand out. Embrace these strategies to enhance your eBook's success and reach a wider audience.

Chapter 21. Writing Book Introductions

Discover how to captivate readers from the very first lines and boost your book sales. A well-crafted introduction is key to hooking your audience and setting the tone for the rest of your book. In this chapter, we'll guide you through a seven-step process to create compelling introductions using ChatGPT. By mastering these techniques, you'll ensure your book stands out and resonates with your target audience from the outset.

Step 1: Understand the book's content and objectives

Understanding your book's content and objectives ensures that you convey the essence of your book effectively. This step is crucial for crafting an introduction that accurately represents your book's value proposition, making it more appealing to potential readers. It helps ensure the introduction is aligned with the overall tone and direction of the book, providing a cohesive reading experience.

- Example Prompt: *"Act as a strategic business consultant. Analyze the core content and primary objectives of 'Startup Success Blueprint' and distill them into a compelling summary that highlights the book's unique value proposition for aspiring entrepreneurs. Here is the content: [Inser the content]"*

Step 2: Identify your target audience

Identifying your target audience ensures that your introduction speaks directly to the people who will benefit most from your book. This step helps tailor your message to address their specific needs, challenges, and aspirations, making your book more relevant and engaging. Knowing your audience allows you to use language and examples that will most effectively capture their interest.

- Example Prompt: *"Act as a market strategist. Profile the ideal target audience for 'Startup Success Blueprint,' detailing their demographics, key motivations, and pain points. Ensure your analysis aligns with the book's objectives to maximize relevance and engagement."*

Step 3: Create thought-provoking questions and issues

Creating thought-provoking questions engages readers by sparking their curiosity and interest. This step encourages them to think about the topics your book will cover, increasing their desire to read more and find answers to these questions within your book. It sets the stage for an interactive reading experience, where readers feel directly involved in exploring the content.

- Example Prompt: *"Act as an entrepreneurial thought leader. Formulate three provocative questions that challenge aspiring entrepreneurs to rethink their strategies, using insights from 'Startup Success Blueprint' as the basis."*

Step 4: Use ChatGPT to draft the book introduction

Using ChatGPT to draft the book introduction leverages AI to generate engaging, high-quality content efficiently. This step ensures that your introduction is compelling, well-structured, and tailored to captivate your target audience from the outset. It also helps in maintaining a consistent tone and style throughout the introduction, aligning with the rest of the book.

- Example Prompt: *"Act as an entrepreneurial mentor. Draft an engaging introduction for 'Startup Success Blueprint' that opens with a compelling challenge or scenario, designed to resonate deeply with aspiring entrepreneurs. Ensure the tone is both inspiring and practical."*

Step 5: Review and edit

Reviewing and editing the introduction ensures clarity, coherence, and alignment with your vision. This step refines the content to enhance its impact, ensuring it effectively engages and resonates with your target audience. It helps in identifying any gaps, redundancies, or inconsistencies, thus polishing the final output.

- Example Prompt: *"Act as a seasoned editor. Critically evaluate the introduction for 'Startup Success Blueprint,' focusing on enhancing clarity, flow, and reader engagement. Suggest specific revisions to ensure the introduction aligns perfectly with the book's target audience and objectives."*

Step 6: Add a personal touch

Adding a personal touch humanizes your introduction, making it more relatable and authentic. This step builds a connection with readers, enhancing the credibility of your book and encouraging them to trust and engage with your content. Personal anecdotes or testimonials can significantly increase the persuasiveness and relatability of your introduction.

- Example Prompt: *"Act as a business mentor. Weave in a personal anecdote or lesson from a entrepreneurial journey that aligns with the themes of 'Startup Success Blueprint.' Ensure this personal touch adds authenticity and strengthens the connection with the reader."*

Step 7: End with a strong call to action

Ending with a strong call to action motivates readers to take immediate steps, such as purchasing your book or exploring its content further. This step is essential for converting interest into action, driving sales, and engagement. A well-crafted call to action can significantly boost your book's visibility and reader engagement.

- Example Prompt: *"Act as a persuasive copywriter. Craft a compelling call to action that encourages readers to dive into 'Startup Success Blueprint' and start implementing its strategies immediately. Ensure the call to action creates urgency and clearly outlines the benefits of taking the next step."*

Illustrative Example:

Step 1: Understanding the book's content and objectives

- Example Prompt: *"Act as a literary expert specializing in historical fiction. Provide an in-depth analysis of the main themes and objectives of the novel 'Echoes of the Past,' focusing on how they shape the narrative and reader experience."*

Step 2: Identifying the target audience

- Example Prompt: *"Act as a book marketing strategist. Define the ideal target audience for the poetry collection 'Whispers of the Soul,' considering demographics, interests, and reading habits that align with the book's themes of love and loss."*

Step 3: Creating thought-provoking questions

- Example Prompt: *"Act as a literary critic. Formulate three thought-provoking questions that could spark discussion in a book club about 'The Silent Woods,' focusing on the protagonist's moral dilemmas."*

Step 4: Drafting the Introduction

- Example Prompt: *"Act as a seasoned author. Draft a compelling introduction for the memoir 'Journey Through Shadows,' opening with a powerful anecdote that captures the reader's attention and sets the tone for the emotional journey ahead."*

Step 5: Reviewing and editing

- Example Prompt: *"Act as a professional editor with expertise in literary fiction. Review and refine the introduction to the novel 'Beneath the Surface,' ensuring that it captivates the reader while maintaining coherence and a consistent narrative voice."*

Step 6: Adding a personal touch

- Example Prompt: *"Act as a memoir writing coach. Weave in a personal story from my experience as a war correspondent to add depth and authenticity to the introduction of my memoir 'Through the Eyes of Conflict.'"*

Step 7: Strong call to action

- Example Prompt: *"Act as a persuasive copywriter. Craft a compelling call to action for the self-help book 'Empower Your Mind,' encouraging readers to take immediate steps toward personal transformation after reading the introduction."*

Creating an engaging book introduction is essential for capturing the interest of potential readers and boosting your book sales. By following this seven-step guide and leveraging the power of ChatGPT, you can craft introductions that are compelling, persuasive, and tailored to your target audience. Embrace these strategies to enhance your book's appeal and reach a wider audience.

Chapter 22. Editing & Revising

Discover the secrets to turning ChatGPT into an excellent assistant for reviewing and editing your book's content. In the fast-paced realm of artificial intelligence, ChatGPT stands out as a vital resource for authors. By mastering how to use ChatGPT for reviewing and editing, you can significantly enhance your book's content. Here's a step-by-step guide to help you leverage ChatGPT for proofreading and editing:

Step 1: Prepare your content

Preparing your content thoroughly ensures that the ideas you present are coherent and engaging. By organizing your manuscript into smaller sections, you make it easier for ChatGPT to provide focused and detailed feedback. This initial preparation sets the foundation for a more effective and efficient editing process.

- Example Prompt: *"Act as a content strategist. Help me divide my manuscript on personal development into logical sections for a more structured review, ensuring each section covers a coherent theme."*

Step 2: Utilize ChatGPT for content review

Utilizing ChatGPT for content review allows you to identify and correct errors in spelling, grammar, and syntax. This step helps you catch mistakes that might have been overlooked and ensures that your text is polished and professional. By being specific in your prompts, you can get targeted and detailed feedback from ChatGPT, enhancing the overall quality of your manuscript.

- Example Prompt: *"Act as a professional editor. Perform a detailed grammar and syntax check on the following passage, ensuring the language is polished and professional: 'Today, I went to buy books at the bookstore near my home...'"*

Step 3: Edit based on ChatGPT's suggestions

Review the suggestions provided by ChatGPT and implement them in your manuscript. Editing based on ChatGPT's suggestions ensures that your content is refined and improved. This step helps you enhance clarity, coherence, and readability while maintaining the original intent of your text. It allows you to make precise corrections and improvements, leading to a more polished and professional manuscript.

- Example Prompt: *"Act as a professional editor. Enhance the clarity and impact of this sentence while maintaining its original meaning: 'He is someone who never gives up, always striving to achieve his goals.'"*

Step 4: Iterate the review process

Iterating the review process allows you to continuously improve your manuscript until it reaches the desired quality. This step ensures that your book is thoroughly reviewed and refined, making it as error-free and engaging as possible. Repetition helps you catch subtle issues and make incremental improvements, leading to a superior final product.

- Example Prompt: *"Act as a professional editor. Conduct a second review of this revised text, focusing on refining sentence structure and flow: 'Finally, she decided to accept the invitation and join their project...'"*

Step 5: Conduct an overall assessment

Conducting an overall assessment ensures that your manuscript is cohesive and well-structured. This step helps you identify any inconsistencies or gaps in the narrative, ensuring a smooth and engaging reading experience. By refining the structure and flow, you enhance the overall impact and readability of your book.

- Example Prompt: *"Act as a professional editor. Help me evaluate the overall structure of my story. My story starts with an adventure, followed by an unexpected meeting, and ends with an intense battle."*

Step 6: Gather feedback from others

Gathering feedback from others provides you with diverse perspectives and insights, helping you identify areas for improvement that you might have missed. This step enriches your manuscript by incorporating valuable suggestions and ensuring that your book resonates with a broader audience. By refining your work based on external feedback, you enhance its overall quality and appeal.

- Example Prompt: *"Act as a professional editor. A peer suggested that the main character in my story needs to express more emotions. Can you provide examples of how to depict this effectively, especially during key moments of conflict?"*

Illustrative Example:

Step 1 – Use ChatGPT for content review

- Example Prompt: *"Act as a professional editor. Check for spelling and grammar errors in the following text: 'They had a long day filled with joy and interesting memories...'"*

Step 2 – Edit the content

- Example Prompt: *"Act as a professional editor. Help me improve this sentence: 'She is a very talented person, always creative and seeking ways to solve problems.'"*

Step 3 – Repeat the process

- Example Prompt: *"Act as a professional editor. Review the following text again and suggest improvements: 'He never thought that one day they would meet again in such a remote place...'"*

Step 4 – Overall assessment

- Example Prompt: *"Act as a professional editor. Help me reevaluate the structure of my story in a general context. My story begins with a romantic relationship, followed by a breakup, and ends with a reconciliation."*

Step 5 – Receive feedback from others

- Example Prompt: *"Act as a professional editor. A friend of mine suggested that the secondary character in my story needs more defined development. Can you provide some examples of how I can achieve this?"*

By following these steps and using these examples, you can effectively use ChatGPT to review and edit your book's content, ensuring a polished and professional final product. Remember, the key is to be patient, creative, and persistent throughout the process to make the most of ChatGPT's capabilities.

Chapter 23. Domain-Specific Examples

Learn how to elevate your book's content by using ChatGPT to generate detailed, domain-specific examples. In this chapter, we'll explore how focusing on specialized fields like healthcare, finance, and marketing can enhance the credibility and relevance of your writing. By mastering these techniques, you'll be able to leverage AI to produce precise, expert-level content that resonates with your target audience and meets their expectations

Example 1: Healthcare

- Prompt Example: *"Act as an experienced endocrinologist. Create a comprehensive treatment plan for managing Type 2 Diabetes, incorporating personalized lifestyle changes, a tailored medication regimen, and a structured follow-up care schedule. Include peer-reviewed citations to support your recommendations and ensure accuracy."*

Example 2: Financial planning

- Prompt Example: *"Act as a certified financial planner. Design a retirement savings plan for a 40-year-old client with the goal of retiring at 65. Include diversified investment strategies, risk mitigation techniques, and a timeline for periodic financial reviews. Back your plan with current financial data and references from trusted sources."*

Example 3: Marketing strategy

- Prompt Example: *"Act as a senior marketing strategist. Formulate a comprehensive marketing strategy for launching a new eco-friendly skincare product line. Define the target demographic, select the most effective marketing channels, craft compelling key messages, and outline measurable success metrics. Ensure your strategy is supported by case studies or industry benchmarks."*

Ensure your prompts are clear and detailed to get the most accurate responses from ChatGPT. Don't hesitate to refine and iterate on the generated content to ensure it meets your needs. Always tailor the generated examples to fit the specific context and audience of your book.

Chapter 24. Text Summarization

Discover how to effectively utilize ChatGPT to create concise, high-quality text summaries that enhance your content's readability and impact. In this chapter, we'll cover techniques to help you master text summarization, making your writing more accessible and engaging for your audience.

Whether you're condensing scientific articles, historical documents, business reports, legal texts, or technical manuals, the strategies provided here will ensure your summaries are precise, well-structured, and aligned with professional standards.

Step 1: Provide context and clear instructions

To get the best results from ChatGPT, start by providing clear and specific instructions about what you need. Specify the desired length, the key points to focus on, and any particular style or tone you want the summary to reflect. This clarity will help ChatGPT deliver a summary that meets your expectations.

- Example Prompt: *"Please summarize the following research paper into a concise paragraph of about 100 words. Focus on distilling the main arguments, methodology, and key conclusions, ensuring the summary is clear and accessible to readers with a general interest in the topic. Here is the paper: [Insert full research paper content]"*

Step 2: Insert text content to be summarized

Next, input the complete text that needs summarizing. Ensure the content is well-structured and clearly articulated, as this will help ChatGPT identify and extract the most important points.

- Example Prompt: *"Summarize the following article on the impact of social media on mental health into a concise paragraph of about 120 words. Emphasize the major findings and implications while making the summary engaging and easy to understand for a broad audience. Here is the article: [Insert full article content]"*

Step 3: Review and edit the results

Once ChatGPT provides the summary, review it thoroughly to ensure it captures the essential points accurately and meets your expectations. If necessary, ask ChatGPT to revise the summary, focusing on any areas that need improvement.

- Example Prompt: *"Please review this summary of the legal brief on intellectual property rights and include more specific details about the case outcomes and their broader legal implications. Here is the initial summary: [Insert summary content]"*

Step 4: Repeat the process if needed

If the summary is not yet satisfactory, provide specific feedback and repeat the process until the summary meets your standards. Continuous refinement is key to achieving a polished and professional summary.

- Example Prompt: *"Please revise the summary of the economic report to better emphasize the key financial trends and strategic recommendations. Ensure the revision highlights actionable insights for stakeholders. Here is the current summary: [Insert summary content]"*

Illustrative Examples

Example 1: Summarizing a scientific article

- Example Prompt: *"Please summarize the following scientific article into a concise paragraph of about 150 words. Distill complex scientific information into a clear and concise summary, making it accessible to a broader audience. Here is the article: [Insert full article content]"*

Example 2: Summarizing a historical document

- Example Prompt: *"Summarize the following historical document on the signing of the Declaration of Independence into a concise paragraph of about 200 words. Preserve the essence of significant events while making the information more accessible and digestible for readers. Here is the content of the document: [Insert full document]"*

Example 3: Summarizing a business report

- Example Prompt: *"Summarize the following quarterly business report into a concise paragraph of about 100 words. Business summaries distill complex financial data into actionable insights, enabling quick decision-making and strategic planning.Here is the content of the report: [Insert full report content]"*

Example 4: Summarizing a legal document

- Example Prompt: *"Summarize the following legal document on the new data privacy regulations into a concise paragraph of about 150 words. Legal document summaries simplify complex legal language, making the regulations more understandable and actionable for non-experts. Here is the content of the document: [Insert full document content]"*

Example 5: Summarizing a technical manual

- Example Prompt: *"Summarize the following technical manual on operating a 3D printer into a concise paragraph of about 120 words. Summarizing technical manuals helps condense detailed operational instructions into a format that is easy to follow, ensuring users can quickly understand and apply the information. Here is the content of the manual: [Insert full manual content]"*

By mastering the techniques outlined in this chapter, you can effectively use ChatGPT to produce high-quality text summaries that enhance the readability and impact of your content. Whether summarizing complex scientific articles, historical documents, business reports, legal texts, or technical manuals, the right approach to text summarization can significantly elevate the quality of your writing.

Chapter 25. Content Repurposing

The purpose of this chapter is to guide you in leveraging ChatGPT for efficient content repurposing, ensuring your material resonates with diverse audiences across various platforms. By mastering the techniques outlined here, you will be able to extend the lifespan of your content, amplify your message, and maximize your reach.

This chapter emphasizes the importance of clarity in prompts, iterative refinement, and contextual relevance, equipping you with the skills needed to adapt your content seamlessly for different platforms while maintaining its integrity and appeal.

Step 1: Repurposing content for Linkedin

LinkedIn is a professional network, and content shared on this platform should be concise, informative, and relevant to professionals. When repurposing content for LinkedIn, focus on delivering value through insights and actionable advice.

- Example Prompt: *"Act as a social media marketing expert. Generate a LinkedIn post based on the following text: [Insert your book chapter text]. The post should be under 500 characters, include relevant hashtags, and adhere to LinkedIn's best practices. LinkedIn posts should be professional and value-driven. By tailoring my content to this platform, I can effectively engage with a professional audience and build my network."*

Step 2: Repurposing content for Twitter

Twitter's character limit forces you to be brief and to the point. When repurposing content for Twitter, focus on creating short, impactful messages that encourage interaction.

- Example Prompt: *"Act as a social media marketing expert. Create a tweet based on the following key points: [list of key points you want to cover]. The tweet should be no longer than 280 characters and suitable for Twitter sharing. Twitter demands brevity. Crafting a tweet that captures the essence of my content while fitting within the character limit ensures that your message is clear, concise, and engaging."*

Step 3: Repurposing content for Instagram

Instagram is a visual platform where aesthetics and concise messaging are key. When repurposing content for Instagram, focus on creating captions that are inspiring, relatable, and visually aligned with your brand.

- Example Prompt: *"Act as a social media marketing expert. Generate an Instagram caption based on the following idea: [idea or topic of your work]. The caption should be no longer than 150 characters and include relevant emojis and hashtags. Instagram captions should be visually appealing and succinct. By incorporating emojis and relevant hashtags, you can increase engagement and make my content more discoverable."*

Step 4: Creating book ads

Book ads require compelling copy that can grab attention and persuade readers to take action. When using ChatGPT to create ads, focus on crafting a catchy tagline and a strong value proposition.

- Example Prompt: *"Act as a marketing copywriter. Write a short ad for my book, 'The Science of Success.' The ad should be less than 30 words, with a catchy tagline and a compelling reason to buy the book. Effective book ads need to be direct and persuasive, highlighting the key benefits and prompting immediate action from potential readers."*

Step 5: Drafting email announcements

Email marketing allows for more detailed communication with your audience. When drafting an email announcement, focus on clearly conveying the main themes of your book while engaging your readers with a compelling narrative.

- Example Prompt: *"Act as an email marketing expert. Write an email announcing my book, 'The Science of Success,' to my newsletter subscribers. The email should be around 200 words, detailing the main themes and special features. Include subject line suggestions with high open rates. Email announcements allow you to build a deeper connection with me audience by providing more context and encouraging them to take action, such as purchasing my book or sharing the news with others."*

Repurposing content across various platforms is essential for maximizing your book's reach and impact. By leveraging ChatGPT to tailor your content for different audiences and platforms, you can ensure that your message resonates wherever it's shared. The key to successful repurposing lies in clarity, iteration, and relevance—each piece of content should be carefully crafted to meet the unique demands of the platform while staying true to your original message.

Chapter 26. Professional Translation

The purpose of this chapter is to guide you in using ChatGPT as a powerful tool for translating content across different languages. By mastering the strategies outlined here, you can produce translations that are not only accurate but also contextually appropriate, capturing the nuances of the original text.

This chapter aims to enhance your understanding of the translation process with AI, empowering you to use ChatGPT effectively in translating professional documents, creative works, technical manuals, and more.

Step 1: Understand ChatGPT's capabilities

Begin by familiarizing yourself with ChatGPT's translation capabilities and its limitations. Understanding what ChatGPT can and cannot do will help you set realistic expectations and use the tool more effectively.

ChatGPT excels in translating everyday language and formal texts but may struggle with idiomatic expressions or highly specialized terminology. Recognizing these strengths and weaknesses will guide you in crafting better prompts and performing thorough reviews of the translations.

Step 2: Prepare the text for translation

Before feeding the text into ChatGPT, ensure it is well-organized and free of errors. A clear and error-free source text will lead to more accurate translations. If the text contains technical jargon or cultural references, consider simplifying or clarifying these elements to ensure that ChatGPT produces an accurate translation.

Step 3: Craft clear and specific prompts

To get the most accurate translation, provide ChatGPT with clear, detailed prompts. Be specific about the target language and any particular requirements for the translation, such as maintaining a formal tone or focusing on technical accuracy.

- Example Prompt: *"Please translate the following paragraph into Spanish, ensuring the tone remains formal and professional. Focus on maintaining the precision of the financial data and the clarity of the strategic context: 'The quarterly report indicates a 15% increase in revenue, driven by strategic investments in emerging markets.'"*

Step 4: Review and edit the translation

After receiving the translation from ChatGPT, carefully review it to ensure accuracy and contextual appropriateness. Look out for grammatical correctness, proper syntax, and cultural relevance.

- Example Prompt: *"Please review the following Spanish translation for accuracy, ensuring that the tone and imagery match the original text. Suggest any necessary changes to improve clarity, fluency, or cultural relevance: 'El sol se estaba poniendo y el cielo se volvió rojo. Los pájaros cantaban y los niños jugaban afuera.'"*

Step 5: Translate additional sections

Continue translating subsequent sections of your text using the same process. Ensure consistency in tone, style, and terminology throughout the document. For lengthy documents, consider breaking the text into smaller sections and translating them individually. This approach allows for better focus and more manageable reviews.

Step 6: Conduct a comprehensive review

Once the entire text has been translated, perform a thorough review to ensure that the translation is cohesive and free of errors. Focus on the flow, readability, and consistency of the text.

- Example Prompt: *"Review the entire translated document to ensure it flows smoothly and maintains consistency in tone and terminology. A comprehensive review ensures that the translated document is polished and professional, with all sections seamlessly integrated. Highlight any sections that may need revision."*

Step 7: Compare with the original text

Compare the translated content with the original to ensure that the meaning, tone, and nuances are preserved. Make adjustments where necessary to align the translation with the original intent.

- Example Prompt: *"Compare the following translated paragraph with the original English text to ensure it retains the same meaning and tone. Comparing the translation with the original text helps maintain fidelity to the source material, ensuring that the translation is both accurate and authentic. Here is the original text: [Inser original text] and here is its translation: [Insert translation].*

Step 8: Seek feedback from others

Gather feedback from peers, colleagues, or native speakers of the target language. Their insights can help identify subtle errors or areas for improvement that you may have missed. Ask a native speaker to review this translated passage for any nuances or idiomatic expressions that may need adjustment.

Illustrative Examples

Example 1: Translating a business email

- Prompt Example: *"Translate the following business email from English to French. Business emails often require a formal tone and precise language, making it crucial to ensure that the translation conveys the correct level of professionalism. Here is the email: 'Dear Mr. Dubois, I hope this email finds you well. We would like to schedule a meeting to discuss the new project. Please let us know your availability.'"*

Example 2: Translating a technical manual

- Prompt Example: *"Translate the following instructions from a technical manual from English to German. Technical manuals require precise and unambiguous language. Accuracy is paramount to ensure that safety instructions are clearly understood in the translated text. Here is the text: 'Turn off the power before performing maintenance. Ensure all safety protocols are followed.'"*

Purpose: Example 3: Translating marketing copy

- Prompt Example: *"Translate the following marketing copy from English to Italian, ensuring it remains persuasive and engaging. Marketing copy must maintain its persuasive impact and appeal in translation, requiring careful attention to tone and style. See the copy as follows: 'Experience the future of technology with our latest smartphone. Sleek design, powerful performance, and cutting-edge features—all in your hands.'"*

Example 4: Translating a legal document

- Prompt Example: *"Translate the following legal document from English to Spanish, ensuring it remains precise and formal. Legal documents demand precision and formality. Ensuring that legal terminology and phrasing are accurately translated is critical to maintaining the document's integrity. Here is the text: 'The parties agree to the terms outlined in this contract, which shall be binding upon all signatories.'"*

Example 5: Translating a creative work

- Prompt Example: *"Translate the following poem from English to French, preserving its rhythm and emotional tone. Creative works like poetry require sensitivity to rhythm, tone, and emotion, making it important to capture these elements in the translation. Here is the poem: 'The stars above, so bright and free, whisper tales of what could be.'"*

By following these steps, you can effectively use ChatGPT as a professional translation assistant, ensuring that your translated content is accurate, culturally appropriate, and of the highest quality. Remember, the key to successful translation with ChatGPT lies in clear prompts, careful review, and iterative refinement. With practice and attention to detail, you can harness the power of AI to produce professional-grade translations across a variety of languages and contexts.

Chapter 27. Creating Engaging Questions

Unleash the power of ChatGPT to craft engaging questions that will elevate your book and enhance reader interaction. In this chapter, you'll learn how to use AI to create thought-provoking questions that turn a passive reading experience into an active, reflective journey.

Well-crafted questions encourage readers to connect with the material on a deeper level, sharing their insights and engaging with your content in meaningful ways.

Step 1: Immerse yourself in your book's content

Begin by thoroughly understanding your book's content, central themes, and key messages. This foundational knowledge is essential for generating relevant and engaging questions that align with your book's goals and resonate with your target audience.

Step 2: Break down the content into subtopics

By breaking down the content into smaller, manageable sections, you can create questions that are specific to each part of the book, making them more relevant and effective in stimulating thought and discussion.

Step 3: Use ChatGPT to generate questions

For each subtopic, use ChatGPT to create engaging and thought-provoking questions. Ensure the prompts you use are clear and specific to guide ChatGPT in producing relevant and impactful questions.

- Example Prompt: *"Generate five questions related to the subtopic 'Essential Cooking Techniques' in the book 'Mastering the Art of Cooking' that will spark reader curiosity and encourage them to experiment in the kitchen. Generate questions helps explore various angles and depths of the content, creating opportunities for readers to engage more deeply with the material."*

Step 4: Review and refine the questions

After generating a list of questions from ChatGPT, review and edit them to ensure they align with your content and audience. Adjust the questions to accurately reflect the book's themes and to foster meaningful interaction. Taloring the questions to your specific audience is also crucial.

Step 5: Incorporate questions into your book

Decide where to include these questions in your book—either at the end of each chapter or in a dedicated section designed for reader reflection and discussion. This not only enhances interaction but also helps readers feel more connected to the content.

Step 6: Gather reader feedback

Once your book is published, actively seek feedback from readers regarding the questions. Consider creating online discussion forums, social media groups, or even hosting live discussions to gather insights and engage with your audience.

Step 7: Refine and update the questions

Continuous improvement of your questions, based on real-world feedback, helps maintain the relevance and appeal of your book over time. This iterative process is key to keeping your content engaging and aligned with the evolving interests of your readers.

Illustrative Examples

Example 1: "Mastering the Art of Cooking"
Subtopic: Essential Cooking Techniques

Step 3: Use ChatGPT to generate questions

- Example Prompt: *"Please generate five thought-provoking questions related to the subtopic 'Essential Cooking Techniques' in the book 'Mastering the Art of Cooking.' Ensure these questions are designed to spark reader curiosity, encourage hands-on experimentation in the kitchen, and inspire deeper engagement with the content."*

Step 4: Review and edit questions

These questions align well with the subtopic "Essential Cooking Techniques" and are likely to engage readers by encouraging them to reflect on their culinary practices and experiment with new techniques.

Step 5: Incorporate questions into the book

At the end of the chapter "Essential Cooking Techniques," include a "Discussion Questions" section featuring these questions to promote reader interaction.

Example 2: "Mindfulness for a Better Life"
Subtopic: Practicing Mindfulness in Daily Life

Step 3: Use ChatGPT to generate questions

- Example Prompt: "Create three interactive and thought-provoking questions about 'Practicing Mindfulness in Daily Life' in the book 'Mindfulness for a Better Life' to encourage reader reflection and discussion."

Step 4: Review and edit questions
These questions are well-suited to the subtopic "Practicing Mindfulness in Daily Life" and encourage readers to think critically about how mindfulness can be integrated into their everyday lives.

Step 5: Incorporate questions into the book
At the end of the chapter "Practicing Mindfulness in Daily Life," include these questions to foster a deeper connection with the content.

Example 3: "Leadership in Action"
Subtopic: Building effective teams

Step 3: Use ChatGPT to generate questions

- Example Prompt: *"Please generate four interactive and engaging questions about 'Building Effective Teams' in the book 'Leadership in Action.' Ensure these questions are crafted to stimulate deep reader reflection, provoke thoughtful discussion, and encourage readers to apply effective team-building strategies in real-world leadership scenarios."*

Step 4: Review and edit questions
These questions are tailored to the subtopic "Building Effective Teams" and are designed to prompt readers to reflect on their leadership practices and team dynamics.

Step 5: Incorporate questions into the book
Include these questions at the end of the "Building Effective Teams" chapter to encourage readers to think critically about their approach to leadership.

These examples illustrate how to effectively use ChatGPT to generate engaging and relevant questions for your book. Tailoring the questions to fit the context and audience of your book is essential for maximizing their impact. By following these steps, you can leverage the power of ChatGPT to create a bestselling, engaging, and interactive book that not only informs but also inspires your readers to reflect, discuss, and apply the knowledge they gain.

Chapter 28. Designing Book Covers

Harness the creative potential of ChatGPT to design captivating book covers that draw readers in at first glance. In this chapter, you'll discover how to use AI to generate and refine design concepts that not only capture attention but also convey the essence of your book.

By aligning your cover with your target audience and genre trends, you can create a visually compelling design that resonates with potential readers. Emphasis is placed on the importance of iteration and feedback, ensuring your final cover is polished, professional, and market-ready.

Step 1: Understand your book's theme and target audience

Begin by developing a deep understanding of your book's theme and target audience. This foundational step ensures that your cover design will resonate with the right readers and effectively convey your book's message.

For example, If your book is a mystery novel targeting young adults, the cover should evoke feelings of suspense and intrigue while appealing to younger readers with a modern, edgy design.

Step 2: Research book cover trends

Explore current trends in book cover design, especially within your genre. Platforms like Pinterest, Goodreads, and Amazon can provide insights into what styles and elements are popular and effective in capturing reader interest.

For example, for a romance novel, you might notice trends like minimalist designs, soft pastel colors, or illustrated covers featuring romantic elements, which you can then incorporate into your design ideas.

Step 3: Use ChatGPT to brainstorm design concepts

With a clear understanding of your book's theme, target audience, and current design trends, use ChatGPT to brainstorm creative ideas for your book cover. Be specific in your prompts to get the most relevant and imaginative suggestions.

- Prompt Example: *"Act as a cover book designer. Please generate five creative book cover concepts for a mystery novel targeting young adults. Ensure each design evokes a strong sense of suspense and intrigue, with visual elements that resonate with the adventurous and curious nature of the target audience. The book cover concepts should be visually appealing, capturing the essence of the mystery genre while also appealing to young adult readers."*

Step 4: Refine your ideas

Review the suggestions provided by ChatGPT and refine them to better fit your vision. Combine elements from different ideas or modify them to enhance their appeal and alignment with your book's theme.

For example, you might combine the shadowy figure from the first idea with the foggy forest path from the third idea to create a more complex and intriguing cover design.

Step 5: Create a mock-up

Using design software like Adobe Photoshop, Illustrator, Canva or even ChatGPT, create a mock-up of your book cover based on the refined ideas. This visual representation helps you see how the elements work together and allows you to make adjustments as needed.

- Example Prompt (for DALL-E within ChatGPT): *"Act as a cover book designer. Create a high-resolution book cover mock-up for a mystery novel targeting young adults titled 'The Midnight Enigma.' The cover should evoke a sense of suspense and intrigue, featuring a dark, misty forest as the background, with subtle glowing footprints leading towards a shadowy figure in the distance. The title should be prominently displayed at the top in bold, eerie typography, with the author's name, [Author Name], subtly placed at the bottom. Use a color palette dominated by deep blues and blacks, with hints of silver and purple to add a mysterious and captivating atmosphere. Ensure the design is visually appealing and suitable for a young adult audience, while conveying the essence of a thrilling, mysterious adventure."*

When using AI tools like DALL-E through ChatGPT for creating book covers or other images, be aware that the AI often struggles with accurately rendering text. The text may appear distorted, unclear, or irrelevant.

To avoid these issues, instruct the AI not to include any text in the image. Instead, add text elements—such as the title and author name—using professional design software afterward. This ensures clear, well-integrated typography in your final design.

- Example Prompt (for DALL-E within ChatGPT): *"Create a high-resolution book cover design for a mystery novel targeting young adults titled 'The Midnight Enigma.' The cover should evoke a sense of suspense and intrigue, featuring a dark, misty forest as the background, with subtle glowing footprints leading towards a shadowy figure in the distance. Use a color palette dominated by deep blues and blacks, with hints of silver and purple to add a mysterious and captivating atmosphere. Please exclude any text or typography on the image itself, as the title and author name will be added separately."*

Step 6: Seek feedback

Share your mock-up with friends, family, or colleagues to gather feedback. Ask for their honest opinions on the design's effectiveness in conveying the book's theme and attracting attention.

Step 7: Use ChatGPT for further refinement

Based on the feedback received, use ChatGPT to further refine your cover design. Ask for additional suggestions or ways to improve specific elements to make the cover more appealing and aligned with your vision.

- Prompt Example: *"Please enhance the following book cover concept, which features a shadowy figure on a foggy forest path. Focus on increasing the visual impact while deepening the atmosphere of suspense and mystery."*

Step 8: Finalize your design

After making the necessary refinements, finalize your book cover design. Ensure it is high-quality, visually striking, and that all elements work harmoniously to convey the desired message.

Illustrative Examples

Example 1: Romance novel

Book Title: "A Love to Remember"

- Prompt Example: *"Generate five visually captivating book cover ideas for a romance novel titled 'A Love to Remember,' targeting an adult audience. Each cover should evoke a deep sense of romance and nostalgia, incorporating elements such as soft, warm color palettes, vintage or sepia tones, and symbolic imagery (e.g., handwritten letters, intertwined hands, or classic romantic settings like a Parisian café or a secluded beach at sunset). Ensure the designs subtly convey the timeless nature of love while maintaining an elegant and sophisticated aesthetic."*

Example 2: Science fiction novel

Book Title: "Galactic Odyssey"

- Prompt Example: *"Generate five imaginative and visually striking book cover ideas for a science fiction novel titled 'Galactic Odyssey,' targeting a young adult audience. Each cover should exude a sense of futuristic adventure, incorporating elements like sleek, otherworldly spacecraft, distant galaxies, vibrant cosmic colors, and bold typography. Consider featuring dynamic scenes of interstellar exploration, alien landscapes, or epic space battles. The designs should convey a thrilling journey through the cosmos, balancing the excitement of discovery with the mystery of the unknown, while appealing to the adventurous spirit of young adult readers."*

By mastering these techniques, you can transform ChatGPT into an invaluable assistant in creating visually stunning and engaging book covers. A well-designed cover is crucial in making a strong first impression, attracting readers, and effectively conveying the essence of your book. With the right prompts and iterative refinement, ChatGPT can help you achieve professional-level results that stand out in the crowded marketplace of self-publishing.

Chapter 29. Social Media Marketing

Unlock the power of ChatGPT to elevate your social media marketing efforts and amplify your book's presence online. In this chapter, you'll learn how to use AI to craft compelling content, optimize platform-specific strategies, and effectively engage with your audience. Through practical, actionable steps, you'll discover how to tailor your marketing approach to different social media platforms, maximizing your reach and impact.

By mastering these techniques, you'll streamline your marketing process, saving time while delivering professional results that resonate with your target audience.

Step 1: Research and choose the right social media platform

Before diving into content creation, it's essential to identify the social media platforms where your target audience is most active. This ensures your marketing efforts are directed at the most effective channels, increasing the likelihood of engagement and conversion.

For example, If your book targets entrepreneurs, LinkedIn would be more suitable than Instagram, as it's a platform where professionals network and share industry-related content.

- Prompt Example: *"Act as a social media marketer. Which social media platform is best for promoting a book on entrepreneurship?"*

Step 2: Create engaging content with ChatGPT

Once you've selected the appropriate platforms, use ChatGPT to craft compelling, unique, and engaging content tailored to each one. The content should align with the platform's best practices and resonate with its users.

For example with Twitter, you might create a post that introduces your book with a captivating excerpt, while Instagram might require a visually appealing image accompanied by a succinct, engaging caption.

- Prompt Example: *"Act as a social media marketer. Create a tweet for my book 'The Path to Success,' introducing it with a compelling excerpt."*

Step 3: Utilize the unique features of each platform

Each social media platform offers unique features that can enhance your posts and boost engagement. By leveraging these features—such as hashtags on Twitter, stories on Instagram, or live streaming on Facebook—you can maximize your book's visibility and appeal.

For example with Instagram, consider creating a visually appealing image of your book cover, accompanied by an engaging caption and relevant hashtags. On LinkedIn, a professional article or a video discussing key insights from your book might be more effective.

- Prompt Example: *"Act as a social media marketer. Generate an Instagram caption for my book 'The Path to Success,' including suitable emojis and hashtags."*

Step 4: Engage and expand your network

Interaction is key to building a loyal reader base. Engage with readers, influencers, bloggers, and journalists to broaden your reach. Use ChatGPT to generate interesting questions or prompts that can initiate meaningful conversations and build relationships.

You could ask ChatGPT to craft a question for Twitter aimed at engaging journalists and bloggers, encouraging them to share their thoughts or experiences related to your book's theme.

- Prompt Example: *"Act as a social media marketer. Create a question to ask journalists and bloggers on Twitter about 'The Path to Success.'"*

Step 5: Monitor and evaluate effectiveness

To understand what works best in your marketing strategy, consistently track the performance of your social media campaigns. Utilize platform-specific analytics tools to measure metrics such as views, shares, comments, likes, and overall user engagement.

For example, Facebook Insights can provide detailed analytics on how your posts are performing, helping you to adjust your strategy based on what resonates most with your audience.

- Prompt Example: *"Act as a social media analyst. Considering the goals of increasing engagement and sales for my book, how can I evaluate the effectiveness of my advertising campaign on Facebook? Please focus on key metrics like click-through rates, conversion rates, and audience engagement."*

Step 6: Optimize and adjust strategy

Based on the data collected, refine and optimize your marketing strategy to improve results. Focus on the content types and platforms that drive the most engagement, and be flexible in adapting your approach based on what the analytics reveal.

For example, if your Instagram videos are receiving more engagement than static posts, consider increasing your video content output and experimenting with different formats to see what works best.

- Prompt Example: *"Act as a social media strategist. Considering my goal of attracting more followers, suggest ways to optimize my Instagram book advertising campaign. Please focus on strategies like content creation, hashtag use, and audience engagement."*

Illustrative Examples:

Example 1: 'Healthy Eating Made Easy' on Instagram

Step 1: Research and choose the right social media platform

- Prompt Example: *"Act as a social media marketer. Given the target audience of health-conscious individuals, which social media platform would be most effective for promoting a cookbook titled 'Healthy Eating Made Easy'? Please consider factors like audience demographics, platform engagement, and content format suitability."*

Step 2: Create engaging content with ChatGPT

- Prompt Example: *"Act as a social media marketer. Create an Instagram post introducing the cookbook 'Healthy Eating Made Easy.' The caption should be engaging and tailored to an audience interested in quick, nutritious meals. Include relevant hashtags and an enticing call-to-action to drive interest and engagement."*

Step 3: Utilize each platform's unique features

- Prompt Example: *"Act as a social media marketer. Generate a detailed Instagram story idea for promoting the cookbook 'Healthy Eating Made Easy.' Include a sequence of story frames that guide viewers through a simple, healthy recipe featured in the book. Ensure each frame is visually appealing, incorporates relevant hashtags, and concludes with a call-to-action, such as a swipe-up link to purchase the book."*

Step 4: Engage and expand your network

- Prompt Example: *"Act as a social media marketer. Create an engaging question for Instagram Stories that sparks a discussion about 'Healthy Eating Made Easy.' The question should encourage followers to share their favorite healthy recipes or tips for eating well, while also tying back to the themes and recipes in the book to promote interaction and interest."*

Step 5: Monitor and evaluate effectiveness

- Prompt Example: *"Act as a social media analyst. Provide a detailed strategy for assessing the performance of my Instagram posts. Include specific metrics to track, tools for measurement, and how to interpret the data to optimize future posts."*

Step 6: Optimize and adjust strategy

- Prompt Example: *"Act as a social media strategist. My recent Instagram posts about 'Healthy Eating Made Easy' have been getting low engagement. Based on this context, suggest tailored strategies to increase interaction, including content adjustments, posting times, and hashtag use."*

By mastering these techniques, you can transform ChatGPT into an invaluable assistant for creating comprehensive, accurate, and engaging social media content that effectively markets your book. Tailoring your strategy to each platform's strengths and continuously refining your approach will help you maximize your book's visibility and success.

Chapter 30. Book Promotion Strategies

Harness the power of ChatGPT to revolutionize your book promotion efforts. In this chapter, you'll explore how to use AI to develop innovative and effective strategies that boost your book's visibility and sales. From creating engaging promotional content to optimizing your marketing approach, you'll learn practical methods to connect with your target audience and maximize your book's potential.

By mastering these strategies, you'll be equipped to elevate your book promotion to new heights, ensuring your work reaches and resonates with readers.

Step 1: Identify goals and target audience

Begin by clearly defining your marketing objectives. Are you aiming to boost sales, increase brand recognition, or expand your social media following? Next, identify your target audience based on demographics such as age, gender, interests, and needs.

For example, if your goal is to increase book sales among female readers aged 25-35 interested in personal development, tailor your content to appeal specifically to this group.

- Prompt Example: *"Act as a marketing strategist with expertise in demographic analysis. Identify the key demographics, including age, interests, and online behavior, for promoting a self-help book aimed at women aged 25-35 interested in personal development."*

Step 2: Create engaging content with ChatGPT

Use ChatGPT to generate compelling content, including book introductions, summaries, and memorable quotes that resonate with your audience. Ensure the content is tailored to the platform you are using.

For example, use ChatGPT to draft a Twitter post that introduces your book with a captivating excerpt.

- Prompt Example: *"Act as a book marketer specializing in Twitter. Draft an engaging and emotionally resonant introduction for the book 'The Path to Fulfillment,' focusing on the transformative journey it offers readers in achieving personal success and happiness."*

Step 3: Write PR articles

Leverage ChatGPT to draft PR articles that highlight the book's benefits and value, making it appealing to potential readers and media outlets. This can help you gain media coverage and build credibility.

- Prompt Example: *"Act as a public relations expert. Craft a concise and compelling PR article that introduces 'The Path to Fulfillment,' highlighting its unique benefits and the real-life impact it has had on readers' personal growth.*

Step 4: Create book review content

Generate positive reviews with ChatGPT that highlight the book's strengths and unique value proposition. These reviews can be used on your website, social media, or in promotional materials.

- Prompt Example: *"Act as a book reviewer. Write a detailed and authentic review of 'The Path to Fulfillment,' focusing on how the book's practical advice and inspiring stories have positively influenced your personal growth."*

Step 5: Create social media content

Develop engaging social media posts, including images, videos, quotes, and success stories related to your book. Tailor the content to each platform's unique audience and features.

For example, for Instagram, create a visually appealing image of your book cover, accompanied by an engaging caption and relevant hashtags.

- Prompt Example: *"Act as a social media manager. Create a tweet introducing 'The Path to Fulfillment,' using engaging language that resonates with self-improvement enthusiasts. Include trending and niche hashtags to maximize reach."*

Step 6: Optimize content

Use feedback from readers and reviews to refine and enhance your promotional content. ChatGPT can assist in adjusting your messaging to better align with audience interests and preferences.

- Prompt Example: *"Act as a content strategist. Refine the messaging in 'The Path to Fulfillment' by emphasizing time management strategies that readers have found most valuable, ensuring the content aligns with their needs and interests."*

Step 7: Monitor and evaluate results

Track the performance of your social media campaigns by monitoring views, likes, comments, and shares. Evaluate the effectiveness of your promotion based on metrics like book sales and social media engagement.

For example, use Facebook Insights to analyze the effectiveness of your Facebook posts and adjust your strategy accordingly.

- Prompt Example: *"Act as a marketing analyst. Evaluate the effectiveness of my book promotion campaign on Facebook by analyzing key metrics such as engagement rates, conversion rates, and audience growth over time. Provide insights on how to optimize the campaign based on these metrics."*

Step 8: Optimize and adjust Strategy

Based on your evaluation, optimize your strategy to improve results. Focus on the types of content and platforms that generate the most engagement.

For example, if videos on YouTube generate high engagement, create more high-quality, engaging videos that resonate with your target audience.

- Prompt Example: *"Act as a digital marketing expert. Analyze my current Instagram book promotion strategy and suggest targeted improvements, such as optimizing content types, posting schedules, and engagement tactics, to increase reach and interaction."*

Illustrative Example:

Example 1: 'Delicious Cooking Recipes' on Instagram

Step 1: Identify goals and target audience

- Prompt Example: *"Act as a marketing strategist specializing in culinary niches. Identify the most effective social media platforms for promoting a cookbook titled 'Delicious Cooking Recipes,' considering factors such as visual content appeal and audience engagement potential."*

Step 2: Create engaging content with ChatGPTt

- Prompt Example: *"Act as a content creator with expertise in culinary marketing. Draft an Instagram post introducing 'Delicious Cooking Recipes,' using vivid, descriptive language to evoke the flavors and experiences in the recipes. Include a call-to-action that encourages followers to try the recipes and share their results."*

Step 3: Utilize each platform's unique features

- Prompt Example: *"Act as a social media strategist. Develop an Instagram Story concept for 'Delicious Cooking Recipes' that showcases a step-by-step cooking process from the book. Include interactive elements like polls or swipe-up links to encourage engagement and drive traffic to the book's purchase page."*

Step 4: Engage and expand your network

- Prompt Example: *"Act as a community manager. Create a thought-provoking question for Instagram Stories about 'Delicious Cooking Recipes' that encourages followers to share their own cooking tips or favorite recipes, fostering a sense of community and engagement."*

Step 5: Monitor and Evaluate Results

- Prompt Example: *"Act as a social media analyst. How do I assess the performance of my recent Instagram posts for 'Delicious Cooking Recipes' by analyzing metrics like reach, engagement rate, and follower growth. Provide insights into what content resonates most with the audience and suggest ways to further optimize future posts."*

Step 6: Optimize and adjust strategy

- Prompt Example: *"Act as a digital marketing expert with experience in food content. Evaluate my current Instagram strategy for promoting 'Delicious Cooking Recipes' and recommend specific adjustments, such as optimizing post timing, experimenting with different content formats, and leveraging user-generated content to boost engagement."*

By following these steps, you can leverage ChatGPT to create a robust and effective book promotion strategy, reaching a wider audience and driving higher engagement. Believe in your abilities, strive for excellence, and take pride in your work to achieve remarkable results in your book marketing efforts.

Chapter 31. Building an Author Profile

Unlock the potential of ChatGPT to craft a compelling author profile that stands out. This chapter offers a step-by-step guide to building a professional and engaging author page that enhances your online presence and solidifies your brand.

By effectively utilizing AI, you'll learn how to connect more deeply with your audience, showcasing your work and personality in a way that resonates and leaves a lasting impression.

Step 1: Define the goals and direction of your author page

Start by identifying the primary goals of your author page. Consider what you want to convey about yourself, your work, and your expertise. Define the key elements that should be included, such as your biography, notable works, awards, writing style, career goals, and personal interests.

Example goals:

- Biography: Include your background, education, and any personal experiences that have influenced your writing.
- Notable Works: Highlight your published books, articles, or other significant contributions.
- Awards: Mention any literary or journalism awards you have received.
- Writing Style: Describe your writing style, whether it's narrative, expository, or lyrical.
- Career Goals: Share your aspirations, such as becoming a bestselling author or expanding into new genres.
- Personal Interests: Include hobbies and interests that resonate with your audience, like travel, photography, or cooking.

Step 2: Generate questions based on your goals

Once you've established your goals, create specific questions to ask ChatGPT. These questions will help you gather the content needed to build your author profile.

- Prompt Examples: *"Act as a career coach. Based on my goal to create an engaging author profile, generate five targeted questions that will help me uncover key details about my background, achievements, and writing style. These questions should guide the development of a compelling and authentic author profile that resonates with my target audience."*

Step 3: Use ChatGPT to create content

Input your questions into ChatGPT to receive content suggestions. Edit, combine, and customize these responses to align with your personal style and the message you wish to convey.

- Prompt Examples: *"Act as a professional biography writer. Craft a creative and engaging personal introduction that highlights my unique experiences and passions. Focus on conveying my journey and what drives me, while making it relatable and inspiring for my audience."*

Step 4: Build your author page

Using the content generated by ChatGPT, start constructing your author page. Focus on the layout, design, and color scheme to ensure they match your style and message.

Example Layout Ideas:

- Visual Appeal: Use harmonious color schemes and readable fonts that reflect your personality and genre.
- Content Organization: Arrange your biography, works, and other information in a logical order that guides the reader's experience.
- Navigation: Include a table of contents or menu for easy navigation.
- Visuals: Integrate images, such as book covers and personal photos, to make the page more engaging.

Step 5: Review and optimize your author page

After building your author page, review it for completeness, functionality, and appeal. Optimize it for speed, mobile accessibility, and search engine optimization (SEO). Seek feedback from trusted sources, and use ChatGPT to generate additional suggestions.

- Example Prompt: *"Act as a digital branding expert. Review my author page and provide five detailed suggestions to enhance its effectiveness. Focus on improving the page's design, content, reader engagement, and overall appeal to better connect with my target audience."*

Step 6: Continuously update and enhance your author page

Regularly update your author page with new content about your works and upcoming projects. Use ChatGPT to generate ideas for blog posts, event announcements, and other activities that keep your page dynamic and engaging. Staying current with industry trends can also help you apply fresh ideas to your profile.

- Example Prompt: *"Act as a content strategist. Suggest a unique blog post idea that highlights a key theme or insight from my latest book. The post should be designed to engage my readers and encourage them to explore the book further."*

Step 7: Leverage social media to promote your author page

Promote your author page across social media platforms like Facebook, Twitter, and Instagram. Use ChatGPT to craft engaging posts that drive traffic to your author page and encourage interaction. Ask ChatGPT for strategies to enhance your social media presence.

- Example Prompt: *"Act as a social media marketing expert. Provide a detailed plan with at least three actionable strategies to boost engagement on my author page, focusing on audience interaction, content variety, and timing for optimal reach."*

Illustrative Example:

Step 1: Define goals and direction

- Prompt Example: *"Act as an experienced author page designer. Based on current best practices for authors in the self-help genre, list the key elements that should be included on my author page to effectively showcase my brand and works."*

Step 2: Generate content

- Prompt Example: "Act as a bestselling author and help me craft an engaging introduction for my author page. My goal is to connect with readers who are new to my work in historical fiction. Focus on introducing my unique style and themes."

Step 3: Optimize the content

- Prompt Example: *"Act as a digital marketing strategist. Provide five specific tips to enhance reader engagement on my author page, focusing on interactive elements, content updates, and calls to action."*

By following these steps and effectively utilizing ChatGPT, you can create a professional and captivating author page that resonates with readers and strengthens your personal brand. A well-crafted author profile not only showcases your achievements but also fosters a deeper connection with your audience, leading to long-term success.

Chapter 32. Limitations & Ethics

As you harness the power of ChatGPT to assist in your writing journey, it's essential to recognize both the limitations of this tool and the ethical considerations that come with its use. While ChatGPT offers substantial advantages for content creation, it's not without its constraints.

This chapter explores the key questions and concerns you should keep in mind to ensure responsible and effective use of ChatGPT in your writing endeavors.

Understanding input and output limits

One of the practical considerations when using ChatGPT is the management of input and output lengths.

Input limits: While ChatGPT doesn't impose a strict character limit on prompts, overly long and complex prompts can lead to convoluted or less coherent responses. To optimize the quality of the output, it's best to keep prompts concise and focused. Aim for clarity and specificity in your instructions to guide ChatGPT effectively.

Output limits: ChatGPT can generate extensive responses, but the length can vary depending on the complexity of the prompt and the session settings. If you need a detailed response or a lengthy passage, it's advisable to break your request into smaller, manageable parts. For instance, instead of asking for an entire chapter at once, you can request a specific section or topic and then use prompts like "Continue" if the response gets cut off. This strategy helps maintain coherence and readability.

The role of human authors in the age of AI

A frequent question is whether ChatGPT might eventually replace human authors. The answer is nuanced:

Creativity and contextual understanding: While ChatGPT is adept at generating text based on the data it has been trained on, it lacks the innate creativity, emotional depth, and nuanced understanding that human authors bring to their work. Human writers possess the unique ability to draw from personal experiences, cultural contexts, and intricate emotions—elements that are essential in creating compelling narratives and insightful nonfiction. ChatGPT, therefore, serves as a tool to augment the writing process, offering inspiration, drafts, and structure, but it cannot replicate the unique voice and creativity of human authors.

Accuracy and reliability of ChatGPT's output

When relying on ChatGPT for content, it's crucial to consider the accuracy of the information it provides.

Accuracy: While ChatGPT can generate accurate and informative responses across a wide range of topics, it is not infallible. The model draws from vast amounts of data, but it does not have the ability to verify facts in real-time or provide expert opinions. This is particularly important in specialized fields where precision is paramount. Always cross-check facts and verify information with reliable sources, especially when dealing with critical or specialized content.

Data recency: The data used by ChatGPT is not always up-to-date. While newer versions of the model GPT, have improved access to more recent data, it's still advisable to verify time-sensitive information independently. If your writing involves rapidly evolving fields or current events, supplementary research from up-to-date sources is essential.

Privacy concerns when using ChatGPT

Data privacy: Your interactions with ChatGPT may not be entirely private. While certain versions offer enhanced privacy controls, especially for enterprise users, standard interactions may be stored and used for further training or shared with third parties. If your work involves sensitive or proprietary information, take extra precautions, such as using anonymized data or opting for services that offer stronger data privacy guarantees.

Bias in AI-generated content

Inherent biases: ChatGPT, like all AI models, can reflect the biases present in the data it was trained on. These biases can manifest in various ways, from subtle cultural stereotypes to skewed perspectives on certain issues. It's important to critically evaluate the responses generated by ChatGPT and be vigilant for any bias that might influence the content. As an author, you have a responsibility to ensure that your work remains fair, balanced, and representative of diverse viewpoints.

Ethical use of AI-generated content

Plagiarism and Attribution: When using text generated by ChatGPT, ethical considerations regarding plagiarism are paramount. Presenting AI-generated content as entirely your own work without attribution is unethical and can have serious consequences, including legal repercussions and damage to your professional reputation. If you use content generated by ChatGPT, it's essential to provide proper attribution. This can be done through citations in your bibliography or footnotes, or by including a disclaimer that acknowledges the use of AI tools at the beginning of your book.

Example Disclaimer: "This work includes elements generated by the ChatGPT language model."

By acknowledging the role of AI in your writing, you maintain transparency and uphold the integrity of your work.

Embracing ethical and responsible AI use

Understanding the limitations and ethical considerations of using ChatGPT is crucial for maximizing its benefits while ensuring responsible use. As you integrate AI into your writing process, be mindful of the following:

- Clarity in prompts: Craft clear, concise prompts to guide ChatGPT effectively.
- Accuracy verification: Always verify the information provided by ChatGPT against reliable sources.
- Privacy awareness: Be conscious of data privacy and choose platforms that align with your privacy needs.
- Bias mitigation: Actively work to identify and counteract biases in AI-generated content.

- Ethical attribution: Ensure proper attribution when using AI-generated content to avoid plagiarism.

By adhering to these principles, you can harness the power of ChatGPT to enhance your writing process, while maintaining the ethical standards expected in academic and professional settings. This approach not only enriches the quality and reliability of your work but also preserves the integrity and originality of your creative output.

Chapter 33. Conclusion

As we reach the conclusion of this comprehensive guide on using ChatGPT to write non-fiction books, it's time to reflect on the transformative journey you've embarked on. From generating initial ideas to refining your content, from creating compelling book covers to building a professional author profile, you have explored the multifaceted ways in which ChatGPT can enhance every aspect of your writing process. This journey was not just about mastering a tool; it was about unlocking new dimensions of creativity, efficiency, and impact in your work as an author.

A new era of writing

In the evolving landscape of digital publishing, artificial intelligence has emerged as a powerful ally for writers. ChatGPT, with its ability to generate content, offer creative suggestions, and provide expert guidance, represents a significant leap forward in the art and science of writing. This book has shown you how to harness this technology to streamline your writing process, enrich your content, and ultimately produce works that resonate deeply with your readers.

By now, you've seen firsthand how ChatGPT can assist in every stage of the writing journey:

- Idea generation: ChatGPT helps you brainstorm and refine ideas, ensuring that your book starts with a strong and compelling foundation.
- Content creation: Whether you're writing chapters, developing outlines, or crafting summaries, ChatGPT serves as a reliable co-writer, providing detailed and engaging content tailored to your specific needs.
- Editing and refining: With its ability to review and suggest improvements, ChatGPT enhances the clarity, coherence, and overall quality of your manuscript, helping you polish your work to professional standards.
- Design and presentation: From generating creative ideas for book covers to building a cohesive author profile, ChatGPT ensures that your book is presented in a way that captures attention and communicates your brand effectively.
- Marketing and promotion: ChatGPT supports your marketing efforts by crafting persuasive content for social media, writing compelling book descriptions, and helping you engage with your audience across various platforms.

Each of these steps represents a crucial part of the writing and publishing process, and by leveraging ChatGPT, you've not only saved time but also elevated the quality of your work. The AI's ability to adapt to your style and objectives allows you to maintain your unique voice while benefiting from its vast knowledge and creative potential.

Embracing the future of writing

The power of ChatGPT lies in its versatility. It is not just a tool for generating words on a page; it is a catalyst for creativity, a mentor for refining ideas, and a partner in navigating the complexities of the publishing world. As you continue to explore and utilize ChatGPT in your writing endeavors, you will find that it opens doors to new possibilities, enabling you to experiment with different genres, styles, and formats.

However, it's important to remember that while ChatGPT is a powerful tool, the heart of your work lies in your own creativity and vision. AI can enhance your writing, but it is your unique perspective and voice that will ultimately resonate with readers. The true magic happens when you blend your creative instincts with the capabilities of ChatGPT, producing work that is both deeply personal and universally appealing.

Inspirational takeaways

As you move forward, here are some key takeaways to inspire and guide you in your writing journey:

1. Leverage technology, honor creativity: Use ChatGPT to enhance your writing process, but always stay true to your creative vision. Technology should serve as a support system, not a replacement for your creativity.
2. Continuous learning: The world of AI and writing is constantly evolving. Stay curious and open to learning new ways to use ChatGPT and other tools to enhance your craft.
3. Iterate and improve: Writing is a process of continuous refinement. Use ChatGPT to iterate on your ideas, edit your content, and explore new angles until you achieve the level of quality you desire.
4. Engage with your audience: Remember that writing is a two-way conversation. Use ChatGPT to help you connect with your readers, whether through engaging content, interactive questions, or effective social media strategies.
5. Celebrate your achievements: Writing a book is no small feat. Take pride in your accomplishments, and use ChatGPT to help you share your success with the world, whether through marketing efforts or building your author brand.

Final thoughts

As you close this book, take a moment to reflect on how far you've come. You've not only learned to harness a powerful tool but also deepened your understanding of the writing process itself. ChatGPT is more than just an assistant; it's a gateway to new creative horizons, enabling you to write with greater confidence, efficiency, and impact.

Your journey as a writer is ongoing, and with the skills and insights gained from this book, you are well-equipped to continue creating works that inspire, inform, and captivate your readers. Believe in your abilities, strive for excellence, and remember that the commitment you bring to your craft sets you apart. Your hard work will yield remarkable results, and the stories you have to tell will leave a lasting impact on the world.

As you move forward, let ChatGPT be a trusted companion on your path to literary success. Together, there are no limits to what you can achieve.

Appendix No 1

Unlock the Power of ChatGPT with 193 Tailored Prompts & Formulas!

Ready to elevate your writing game? Dive into a comprehensive collection of 193 expertly crafted prompts and their corresponding formulas, designed specifically for authors looking to harness ChatGPT's full potential.

Why You'll Love This:

- **Save Time:** Get instant access to ready-made prompts that guide ChatGPT to deliver precise and relevant content.
- **Boost Creativity:** Break through writer's block with prompts that spark innovative ideas and fresh perspectives.
- **Streamline Your Process:** Simplify your workflow with prompt formulas that you can adapt and reuse for any project.
- **Achieve Professional Results:** Tailored prompts ensure you get the high-quality content you need, every time.

Simply scan the QR code to access your 193 tailored prompts & formulas.

Appendix No 2

Enhance Your Writing Journey

Would you consider taking a moment to boost your own writing progress? Your insights are powerful.

As you master using ChatGPT for writing, your feedback can reinforce what you've learned and help others on the same path. Sharing your review is more than just a comment—it's a way to solidify your understanding, connect with fellow writers, and contribute to a thriving community.

If this book has inspired you or improved your writing process, please share your thoughts. Your review can:

- Strengthen Your Learning: Reflect on and internalize your new knowledge.
- Connect with Authors: Engage with a network of like-minded writers.
- Support the Community: Guide others to valuable resources.

Enjoyed the book? Scan the QR code to leave a quick review. Your feedback benefits everyone.

Thank you for contributing to our community of AI-powered authors.

We have something else for you!

In a world where AI is transforming every industry, harnessing the power of these tools is crucial to achieving success.

If you're ready to take your writing to the next level and make your first million with ChatGPT, this book is your roadmap.

Scan this QR code to access this book.

Scan the QR code to access our book collection.

www.ingramcontent.com/pod-product-compliance
Lightning Source LLC
LaVergne TN
LVHW060123070326
832902LV00019B/3110